PRAISE FOR
STAN WEBB AND *OPTIMIZE YOUR WEALTH*

"I have known Stan Webb for over six years and we have traveled around the country providing free financial literacy services to help students better manage their money, reduce college costs, and discover employment opportunities. Not only has he given his time free of charge, but he is now working with our board member "The Shark" Daymond John on several financial initiatives that will educate students and young adults about Wall Street, stocks and bonds, entrepreneurship, money management, investment opportunities, and economic development. With Stan and Daymond working together, we will definitely help students and adults achieve their personal, financial, and business goals."

—CHARLES FISHER

Founder of the Hip-Hop Summit Youth Council; Former manager of NCIS TV star and two-time Grammy Award winning artist LL Cool J.

"Stan is truly a force for good. His approach to philanthropic and community engagement is a luminous reflection of the diligence and intensity that characterize his professional endeavors. It was my pleasure to coach Stan during the process of launching the Minerva Foundation for Financial Literacy. The Foundation has become a home for his vision of youth outreach promoting the fundamental financial tenets of personal responsibility and common sense. Stan travels tirelessly to share his expertise and make the subject accessible and comprehensible to children and their communities, partnering with professional athletes, entertainers, and business leaders to create lively and memorable 'teaching moments'."

—LISA ANNE THOMPSON TAYLOR, CGT

Philanthropic Counsel and Certified Governance Trainer

T0122760

OPTIMIZE

your

WEALTH

OPTIMIZE

your

WEALTH

your personal guide to **ENHANCING, PROTECTING,**

and **SUSTAINING** generational wealth

S T A N   W E B B

Published by Advantage, Charleston, South Carolina.
Member of Advantage Media Group.

ADVANTAGE is a registered trademark and the Advantage colophon is a trademark of Advantage Media Group, Inc.

Printed in the United States of America.

ISBN: 978-1-59932-600-9
LCCN: 2015939471

Book design by Megan Elger.

This publication is designed to provide accurate and authoritative information in regard to the subject matter covered. It is sold with the understanding that the publisher is not engaged in rendering legal, accounting, or other professional services. If legal advice or other expert assistance is required, the services of a competent professional person should be sought.

Advantage Media Group is proud to be a part of the Tree Neutral® program. Tree Neutral offsets the number of trees consumed in the production and printing of this book by taking proactive steps such as planting trees in direct proportion to the number of trees used to print books. To learn more about Tree Neutral, please visit **www.treeneutral. com**. To learn more about Advantage's commitment to being a responsible steward of the environment, please visit **www. advantagefamily.com/green**

Advantage Media Group is a publisher of business, self-improvement, and professional development books and online learning. We help entrepreneurs, business leaders, and professionals share their Stories, Passion, and Knowledge to help others Learn & Grow. Do you have a manuscript or book idea that you would like us to consider for publishing? Please visit **advantagefamily.com** or call **1.866.775.1696.**

FOREWORD

There is little question that financial insecurity plagues our society. But fortunately, this plague has a cure: knowledge. *Optimize Your Wealth* presents proven knowledge and practical insights that can strengthen the financial competence of those who embark on this literary journey.

Optimize Your Wealth empowers readers with practical knowledge and actionable strategies. Readers who implement the strategies offered may enjoy increased financial security and the freedom to focus on their passions and on building their legacy.

Enhancing, protecting, and sustaining wealth are the three goals of this book. This book serves as a road map that can help you better navigate the journey to financial wellness and employ your wealth to the fullest when you arrive at your ultimate destination.

Stan Webb is not merely a dispenser of knowledge; he is a veteran financial professional whose mission is to guide readers toward financial wellness. He understands that a "one-size-fits-all" pedagogy does not work for everyone. He astutely addresses the complex subject of personal finance—and the unique emotional reactions it elicits—with keen insight and sensitivity.

Optimize Your Wealth offers ideas and guidance to those who seek to improve their financial planning and wealth management. The insights in this book can help readers make qualified financial decisions that improve their lives, the lives of their loved ones, and the lives of people they influence worldwide.

Vince Shorb, CEO, National Financial Educators Council

> *Vince Shorb is CEO of the National Financial Educators Council (NFEC). Prior to founding the NFEC, Shorb reviewed the personal financial statements of more than 10,000 people across the country. This real-world experience in the financial literacy field contributes to his deep understanding of the challenges people face today.*
>
> *Shorb has been highly acclaimed as a leading financial education authority. He led the development of the National Financial Capability Strategy and was instrumental in the creation of national standards for financial educators and learners. Shorb has been featured* in *CNN Money,* New York Post, *CNBC, Forbes.com, and* The New York Times.

TABLE OF CONTENTS

How Will You Benefit from Reading This Book?

This book was written to help you *optimize your wealth*. It is a how-to guide for achieving three specific objectives:

1. *Enhance* your wealth

2. *Protect* your wealth

3. *Sustain* your wealth

Enhancing wealth is about capitalizing on opportunities. It is about making smart decisions regarding where and how to use your resources for the benefit of you and your family. Some of the best opportunities are not always apparent to the untrained eye. To enhance wealth, you must know what to look for—and where to look for it.

Protecting wealth is about minimizing threats that can adversely affect your wealth. It is about managing risk in a prudent and cost-effective way. Undue risk comes in many forms. It can easily be overlooked until it is too late to avoid. Protecting wealth requires insight and foresight. It demands that you remain diligent and proactive at all times.

Sustaining wealth is about stewardship. It is about managing your resources with an eye toward the future. When it comes to intergenerational wealth, sustainability depends on the extent to which a family's values are passed on from one generation to another. Stewardship calls for a strong sense of purpose. It requires that you maintain a clear and meaningful vision—one that is embraced by those who will carry your torch in the future.

Wealth optimization is a journey rather than a destination—an ongoing process that will help you achieve your goals. It is a discovery process that is enlightening and profitable, providing you with a deeper and broader perspective of your wealth. The ultimate goal of this book is to help you employ your wealth to its fullest.

Optimize Your Wealth Your Personal Guide to Enhancing, Protecting, and Sustaining Generational Wealth consists of nine chapters. Here is a brief summary of what you will find:

Chapter 1: Know Thy Wealth

"The essence of knowledge is self-knowledge," said Plato. In order to optimize one's wealth, one must know oneself, as well as one's wealth. The first step is to get very clear about what wealth means to you.

You should understand what you want your wealth to do for you and those closest to you. In Chapter 1, you learn how to ask yourself excellent questions about what wealth means to you. Clarity comes from asking better questions. When you ask better questions, you gain deeper insights. Deeper insights allow you to make smarter decisions.

Chapter 2: The Psychology of Money

In this chapter you learn how your beliefs, expectations, feelings, and attitudes toward money affect your financial behavior and outcomes. The psychological factors that affect how we interact with money can have a powerful effect on our end results. In fact, our mind and emotions can have a more powerful effect on our financial outcomes than how much money we have.

Chapter 3: Use an Integrative Approach

To *optimize* your wealth, you should also adopt a broader perspective by considering the many factors that can impact your wealth, both positively and negatively. In Chapter 3, you learn about an integrative approach that will enable you to do just that.

Chapter 4: Check Your Assumptions

The number of ideas about what you should do with your money is exceeded only by the number of people trying to sell you on those ideas. In Chapter 4, you learn how to separate the wheat from the chaff when it comes to financial advice. To do that, you must understand how the financial services industry operates, build your knowledge base, surround yourself with experts, and then boldly and continually question the assumptions that both you and your experts hold!

Chapter 5: Keep an Eye on the Future

Optimizing your wealth is about maximizing opportunities and minimizing threats. To accomplish this, you need to *identify* hidden opportunities and unexposed threats. In chapter 5, you learn how to do that by applying some valuable techniques that will enable you and your family to anticipate future needs and high-impact events that can affect your wealth optimization goals.

Chapter 6: Get Your Family Involved

One of the costliest mistakes you can make is not talking to your family members about financial matters. In chapter 6, you learn why involving your entire family is essential to optimizing your wealth. You learn how to identify those family members who play a vital role in your wealth management plan, whether because they are in a position to leave you with wealth, inherit your wealth, or help build your wealth.

Chapter 7: Strive for Stewardship

Stewardship is an essential concept in optimizing generational wealth. In chapter 7, you learn how to embrace a "sustainability mindset" and become a more effective steward of your family's wealth. You also develop strategies for instilling these values in other family members.

Chapter 8: Leave a Meaningful Legacy

Most people strive to leave a meaningful and lasting legacy. Unfortunately, not everyone knows how to go about accomplishing that goal. In chapter 8, you will assess your own legacy plan to determine whether your plan aligns with your values and desires. You also gain some tips on how to create a more powerful legacy, as well as how to encourage your friends and family to do the same.

Chapter 9: Building Your Team

In chapter 9, we will talk about how to build a wealth management team. You will learn about important concepts and things to consider before you put the team together or choose a team leader. Sometimes the advisors you now have may not work with your new dynamic wealth optimization plan. You may recognize that they are really nice people but more transaction orientated than you thought before reading this book. If they always have something you need to buy or have applications in hand every time you get together, are they the right leader or even a team member? Transaction-oriented people may not be the best for your long-term team made up of people on your side first. Your new team should be a team of experts that will look out for you in all aspects of your plan. I am a firm believer that strong, slow, and steady is better than jumping first and then seeing later where you land. You will learn that the psychological profile match is imperative.

THROUGH THE LENS OF EXPERIENCE: *INSIGHTS ON WEALTH*

Throughout the book, you will find perspectives on wealth from experienced individuals. Entitled "Through the Lens of Experience: Insights on Wealth," these interviews share the wisdom and experience of successful individuals.

Why I Wrote This Book

As a young child growing up in rural North Georgia, I developed a unique perspective about money. My parents were far from wealthy. They were modest people, both emotionally and financially. Although we never went hungry, we certainly did not have any extra funds to go around at the end of the month.

My parents knew nothing about investing, but they were savers. When I was about 12, my dad took me down to the local bank and helped me open my first savings account. From that point on, the bank manager called me "Little Webb." Shortly after that, I developed a life-threatening illness, and then a year after that I was almost killed in an automobile accident.

For several years, I spent a lot of time in hospitals and doctors' offices and developed a very strong desire to be a doctor. I wanted to help people, just as my own doctors and nurses had helped me. Unfortunately, my personal physician advised me that my condition would prevent me from making it through residency. I was crushed. I really wanted to help people.

After eventually finding my way into the financial services industry, I had a lot of questions about money. The financial services industry was a place to both learn and help others. But I also learned a few lessons from the "school of hard knocks."

When I was in my 20s, I lost almost everything and had to completely rebuild financially. I had opened a business and was a year into it and almost profitable. However, working long hours and weekends was not easy. A friend of mine suggested that we could make a lot of money if we went into the long distance business together. We would both put up some money; he would be the engineer, and I would run the business. I would have to close my business and move to Chicago from the Atlanta area.

As someone who was raised in a rural, working class family, I was taught that people mean what they say and that all you need is someone's word to serve as the foundation for a business transaction. Needless to say, I was very naïve and did not realize how money can distort someone's character.

In one short year, I was completely out of money. My "business partner" had never gotten around to signing our business agreement because, for one thing, he was always changing lawyers, so I had no contract. I had to sell all of my possessions: my house, my car, my boat, and my motorcycle. Fortunately, the equity in the house was just about enough to get me back to zero, but the situation erased about ten years of hard-earned savings.

In reality, I had known that there were risks and that this might not be a good gamble, but the story was good, and the excitement was real. Like many people in similar situations, I let my emotions rule, leading to a very costly decision. As a result I realized that I had a lot more to learn about money, business practices, and human reactions to money—all of which led me to get into this business. My desire to help people now comes from experience, and deep down in my soul that basic mindset has been there since childhood.

In short, *Optimize Your Wealth* was born out of my deep desire to help others. It is my sincere hope that it will accomplish that for you and the people about whom you care most.

Stan T. Webb
Wichita, Kansas
November 2014

CHAPTER ONE

Know Thy Wealth

"Know thyself."

—Inscribed on the forecourt of the
Temple of Apollo at Delphi

Legend has it that the seven sages of ancient Greece—the philosophers, statesmen, and lawgivers who laid the foundation for Western culture—gathered in Delphi to inscribe "Know thyself" at the entry to its sacred oracle. The adage subsequently became a touchstone for Western philosophers and gained even further acceptance as the influence of Greek philosophy expanded through the ages.

The ancient Greek philosophers believed that self-knowledge is a prerequisite to all other forms of knowledge. This ancient wisdom also applies to wealth optimization. That is, before you can optimize your wealth, you must first know thyself *and* thy wealth! No matter your wealth or position in life now, knowing more about both thyself and thy wealth can help you optimize your wealth.

Knowing thyself is important because experiences dating back to childhood materially impact our ability to accumulate and preserve wealth. Knowing thy wealth means knowing the

9

nature and the drivers of your wealth as well as your perception of wealth. A diverse array of factors can significantly affect wealth in positive and negative ways. As wealth advisors, we have found that most people, even those who have accumulated significant wealth, know themselves and their wealth at a very superficial level.

For this reason, I begin every new relationship with a series of conversations that help me understand how well my clients know themselves and how well they know their wealth. In the case of generational wealth—wealth that will survive multiple generations—I also encourage my clients to include family members in these conversations. As you will learn in chapter 7, it is never too early to instill the notion of *stewardship* in the hearts and minds of those who will be influencing or inheriting your hard-earned wealth.

Presented below is a series of questions that will guide you in getting to know yourself and your wealth better. Take your time with these questions and revisit your answers a few times over the next several weeks. As with anything in life, the benefits you derive from this exercise will be based on the amount of effort you put into it.

Getting to Know Thyself

What Did You Learn about Money as a Child?
(More Than You May Think!)
Perceptions of money developed in our formative years may remain with us throughout our lives. So understanding the drivers of your early perceptions of money will help you to understand your current view of money. Reflect on the answers to these questions:

1.   What were your earliest experiences with money?

2. Were those experiences positive or negative?

3. If they were negative, when were your first positive memories?

4. Who were the most influential people in your life when you were growing up?

5. What did they teach you about money?

6. What did you learn from them just by observing what they did with their money?

7. What do you think you learned from those experiences with money?

8. How do you think they have influenced your feelings about money, and do those experiences still influence you when you make decisions about money?

9. Do they influence you in a positive or negative way?

10. If you were to take one major lesson about money learned earlier in life that really had an effect on you, what lesson would it be?

11. What could you learn from your early experiences that you could use today to enhance your wealth?

12. Do any of these experiences pose a risk to your wealth?

How Financially Literate Are You?

Not only should you gain an understanding of your early experiences with money, it is also important to gain an understanding of how financially literate you are. How solid is your grasp of the fundamental principles of sound financial management? How proficient are you in managing your finances?

To help you assess your financial literacy, we are providing you with the test below. The fact that you are willing to take a test shows that you are open to honestly assessing your level of financial knowledge—and taking the steps necessary to improve it.

The test was designed by the National Financial Educators Council (NFEC), a full-service education company that provides financial literacy material, promotes advocacy campaigns, sets standards, conducts research, and shares best practices. To access a wide array of resources, visit the NFEC's Financial Literacy Testing and Survey Center, which provides more than 20 free online tests and survey tools. I am proud to have been asked to be a member of their advisory council and a member of the Personal Finance Speakers Association.

The Advanced Financial Literacy Test can be accessed via this link:

http://www.financialeducatorscouncil.org/
financial-literacy-test/

Once you have completed the test, the website will provide you with a score and an explanation of your level of financial literacy.

THROUGH THE LENS OF EXPERIENCE: *INSIGHTS ON WEALTH*

OPTIMIZE YOUR WEALTH:
You can be successful and not wealthy, and you can be wealthy and not successful. On one hand, I think wealth speaks of money. On the other, I feel wealthy because I have a beautiful wife who loves me very much.

continued on next page.

Getting to Know Thy Wealth

You now have a clearer sense of yourself—your history, your childhood influences, and your concept of wealth— so you can now develop a clearer sense of your wealth. Begin by answering these two questions. Again, take your time and think carefully about your answers.

At what level of net worth would (did) you consider yourself to be wealthy? Why?

What does "wealth" mean to you?

I have been asking those two questions of my clients for more than 20 years and have yet to hear the same answer. Some people whose net worth exceeds $10 million do not consider themselves to be wealthy. Others with far fewer *financial* resources consider themselves to be supremely wealthy.

How can smart people have such divergent views about a seemingly simple concept? The short answer is that the concepts of wealth and of what it means to be wealthy are anything but simple. Wealth is one of the most personal subjects anyone can discuss. For this reason, many people have a strong

continued from previous page.

I work day to day in an office where I'm surrounded by intelligent people who make me a better person and make sure that I work harder. In those senses I would use *wealthy* to describe those feelings. I would use *wealthy* to describe those characteristics of my life.

The best definition of wealth is the set of benefits that we have earned and that we have been blessed with in life. That can be in the form of money. But I suppose it can be in the form of luck or friends.

It is something that you can convey to others too. Something that can be inherited, something that can be shared, something that can be used to benefit those around you... I think it probably comes down to some old proverb about being rich in money and poor in spirit.

Wealth is some combination, difficult to define, of money and the various unique blessings that we all have as individuals.

—*Omar Ashmawy, Entrepreneur*

aversion to thinking and talking about their wealth. However, avoiding the topic of wealth can lead to adverse and unintended consequences for the entire family.

In addition to being highly personal, I have found that people tend to define *wealth* very differently. Many equate wealth with net worth (assets minus liabilities). While easy to measure, this purely financial perspective of wealth can cause a person to overlook some very important *intangible* aspects of wealth, such as their health, their values, and their legacy. Although these intangible aspects of wealth are more difficult to measure, they are in many ways just as important to consider, if not more so. As a wealth advisor, it is crucial for me to truly understand my clients' definitions of intangible wealth. I can then understand the essence of my clients, their goals, and the passion behind their desires.

This book is about helping you to live a more fulfilling life—and to leave a more meaningful legacy. Developing a strong concept of wealth will serve as a guide for you in setting your goals and developing your legacy.

To help you explore your own concept of wealth, reflect on these definitions:

CONCEPTS OF WEALTH

- Wealth is my money working for me rather than me working for money.
- Wealth is having control of my time.
- Wealth is the ability to have a significant impact on the world— even if I live modestly.
- Being wealthy is having an income or assets above _____ (insert number).
- Wealth to me is _____ (insert definition).

As discussed earlier, there are many factors that can affect a family's wealth, both in positive and negative ways. In this chapter, we have dealt with the early influences that have shaped you and your concept of wealth. We have equipped you to "know thyself" and "know thy wealth." For some of you, this may be a review. But do not underestimate the importance of review, as it may enable you to pick up at least one more idea that can add value to the rest of your life and your legacy.

In chapter 2, we explore another vitally important set of factors that influence how you make financial decisions and manage your wealth: your mind and your emotions. Exploring the "psychology of money" is another important step in the process of optimizing your wealth.

CHAPTER TWO

Know *Your* Psychology of Money

"Money is more about mind than it is about math."

—Unknown

In the first chapter, we saw that there are many different concepts and definitions of wealth. Your concept of wealth plays a large role in how you approach financial decisions and wealth management.

In this chapter, we learn about other significant factors affecting your approach to managing money: your mind and your emotions.

Why Emotions Matter

It is well documented that money management is about far more than just math. People make financial decisions at times that defy logic. Their decisions often run counter to what "just the facts" would indicate as the proper course of action. Our mind and emotions play a key role. Indeed, a growing field of behavioral science is the "psychology of money" or the role that emotions, attitudes, previous experiences, and behaviors play in our financial decisions.

What impact do emotions have on our financial decisions? Does it matter that our emotions affect our financial planning?

My experience with clients suggests that indeed, emotions do matter tremendously—and that, unfortunately, emotions often negatively impact our decisions. When people allow fear to dictate the composition of their financial portfolios, they build an overly conservative portfolio and miss out on financial upside. Greed, on the other hand, can lead to overly aggressive financial decisions. Both greed and fear drive the financial markets, and both can lead to poor decisions and outcomes. However, those two emotions are not the only ones that can affect your decisions.

Let's talk about all the emotions involved with money and financial decisions. According to psychologist Robert Plutchik's wheel of emotions theory, there are basically eight emotions, which, like colors on a color wheel, can be expressed at different intensities and mix with one another to create "combination emotions." An emotion's intensity increases as you move toward the center of the wheel and decreases as you move away from it— the darker the shade, the more intense the emotion. For example, rage is the stronger form of annoyance. Just as in colors on a color wheel, each emotion has a polar opposite on the other side of the wheel.

We do not have space in this book to go into more detail about Plutchik's wheel. For the purposes of this discussion, the wheel of emotions is a tool that shows how the different emotions are all connected and how each can make a difference in how you make your financial decisions—or any decision, for that matter. Look at the chart and see how intertwined your emotions can be and how the same emotion can shift into another emotion, depending on the intensity of the initial emotion.

Plutchik's Wheel of Emotions

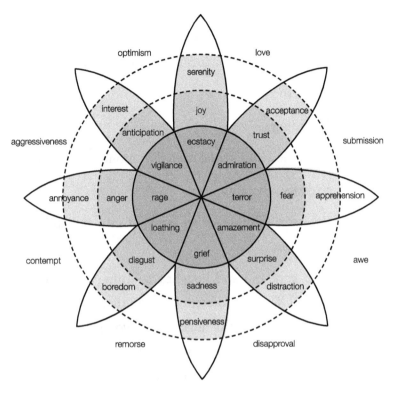

1. **Trust**—includes admiration and acceptance.

2. **Fear**—the feeling of being afraid, shocked, or scared.

3. **Surprise**—how you feel when something unexpected happens.

4. **Sadness**—feeling sad. Other words that describe sadness are sorrow, grief, and depression.

5. **Disgust**—feeling something is wrong or dirty.

6. **Anger**—feeling angry or enraged.

7. **Anticipation**—the sense of looking forward positively to something that is going to happen.

8. **Joy**—feeling happy, glad.

Which of these eight emotions would you say are involved in financial decisions? They all are!

A distortion in any of these emotions can lead to dysfunctional mindsets, attitudes, and behaviors related to money, including:

- Binge spending

- Hoarding

- Deception and denial related to money and spending

- Excessive frugality

- Excessive confidence in one's investment ability and judgment

Have you ever gone out and bought something when you were mad at someone? Was it a different decision than you would have made without the emotion of anger? Have you gone and cruised the mall when you were sad? Bought something at the spur of the moment from a stockbroker because the story was just too exciting to pass up? Moved all of your money out of the market because you were very scared that day and put it somewhere else and then regretted it later because the market went far higher before you got back in?

Most, if not all, of these emotional buys cost you money. In fact, the cost could have been substantial if you missed a nice 5–10 percent move in the market on an investment of hundreds of thousands of dollars.

MIND AND EMOTIONS EXERCISE

1. Which of the following emotions could influence a person to make a poor financial decision?

   a. Fear

   b. Joy

   c. Sadness

   d. All of the above

2. How can you avoid having negative feelings about money?

   a. Delay setting up a savings plan to avoid stress.

   b. Delay setting up a spending plan to avoid arguments.

   c. Think about your dreams and hope everything works out.

   d. Only spend money you have.

3. Cultural values have little effect on the formation of an individual's lifestyle and financial choices.

   a. True

   b. False

4. My personal emotions can be effected by my financial situation.

   a. True

   b. False

5. What decisions have I made before that I know now were probably caused by an emotion?

   _____

   _____

   _____

6. How does my financial situation affect my emotions?

   _____

   _____

   _____

7. How do my emotions affect my financial situation?

_____

_____

_____

8. Why is it important to know how money and emotions affect one another?

_____

_____

_____

To help you recognize how your mind and emotions affect your financial decisions, complete the emotion exercise above. The goal of the exercise is to help you understand *why* you may be making these decisions. Once you are able to recognize an emotion that could result in a poor outcome, you are in a position to manage that emotion for a better outcome.

I always advise my clients to avoid making any financial decisions in the immediate aftermath of major life events, such as death, divorce, and job loss. It is important to first bring balance and clarity to the decision. Trusted professional advisors who are truly looking out for your best interest can bring balanced emotions and logic to a difficult situation. Your team is there to help you through any crisis that may involve your finances. A strong advisor should know you, your personality, your goals, and your risk profile—not just the performance of your investment portfolio. I know that at DreamCatcher Wealth Management, my company, we have found that the better we know our clients, the more we are able to help them. Getting through difficult financial times can be hard, but many times we are able to lessen the blow. We get great pleasure in helping our clients in good and bad times.

The importance of aligning your mind, your emotions, and your money cannot be overestimated. Even if you are very intelligent, if you lack an understanding of your "money personality," you may allow your emotions to cloud your judgment, resulting in poor financial decisions.

What to Do

Given how susceptible we are to our emotions, what are we to do? Can we eliminate all emotion? That's impossible. We are human, after all—we will always be subject to our emotions to a certain extent. However, it is important to take the following steps to minimize the negative impact of your mind and emotions on your wealth management:

1. Educate yourself. Become more financially literate.
Although math does not always trump emotions, it is important to have a base of financial knowledge to help you make sound decisions, which is why we provided you with the Financial Literacy Test in chapter 1. When emotions are raging, sometimes a base of financial knowledge can provide the voice of reason that you need to prevail over the emotions of the moment.

2. Know your emotional triggers and responses.
What are your emotional triggers? What are your reactions? Why do you have them? Learn to recognize the triggers and reactions—and the reasons. This insight will help you to better manage habits and tendencies that may prevent you from optimizing your wealth.

Start with your past. Stopping for a moment and thinking back to your first experiences with money, and the emotions you carry from that, will help you today. Examples could be anything from being raised in a poor environment and always having to struggle with bills, to having someone in the family always chasing dreams that caused the family to struggle with money, to just spending time with a grandparent who taught you little things about money that you carried forward.

Building on the knowledge of your early experiences with money, examine your current attitudes toward money. How do you approach financial decisions now?

Often events and people influence us in ways we don't recognize or even remember but still have a profound influence on our lives, both positive and negative. A little exploration into why you do some of the things you do with money will help you move forward in the direction you want to go.

According to Meir Statman, a behavioral finance expert at Santa Clara University, and Vincent Wood, president of a behavioral research and testing firm in San Francisco, there are basically four types of personalities in money matters.

PERSONALITY TYPE	BEHAVIOR
Guardians	Cautious with their money
Artisans	Freewheeling and daring
Idealists	Care less about money than other goals
Rationals	Make most decisions by the numbers

Although most people are mixtures of these types, Statman and Wood's research shows that most people lean strongly toward one or, at most, two of the categories. Once you know your type(s), you can better defend yourself against your weaknesses and take advantage of your strengths.

I encourage my clients to identify which of these personality types they lean toward, because that knowledge helps in making a wealth optimization plan that they can be comfortable with. If you are disciplined and bold and place a high importance on wealth, you are going to be interested in very different options than an Idealist, who places less priority on managing money and prefers to go a less risky route. You may have attributes from more than one of the personality types. Being disciplined (Rational) and bold (Artisan) can mean you try to use the numbers to rationalize money decisions but couldn't care less about having and making more wealth, so that it is more about just enjoying the journey.

I often work with people who really fit into one or two of the different categories. Most of the time, if a couple comes in, all four of the personality types could be in play, which makes their family dynamic and the financial plan more complex. Let's say that one of the couple was raised during the Depression. There is a good chance they will have some of the Guardian behavior, but let's say that they are married to someone who is more of an Artisan and is a little more willing to take risks and is more freewheeling in decision making. Discussing personality types can be extremely enlightening for the couple. It is rare for an advisor to get into this much detail on first acquaintance with clients and to take the extra time to truly understand the clients they are supposed to serve.

Recently, a couple that came to see me had one Guardian personality and one strong Rational personality. If we look at just the personality types, this could be a difficult match. The wife (a Guardian) was a super saver, and the husband, an engineer, was a

Rational, who would only make financial moves if he could justify the numbers. I spoke with them about their past and why they thought of money the way they did, and they said no one had ever approached their finances that way before.

Through this process, we uncovered why the wife was so afraid of doing anything and why the husband was willing to do just about anything if the numbers were there, without regard to her fears. We were able to find common ground between them in decisions about money and a way for them to move forward in a more organized way—a way that was safer to the Guardian but that made enough returns to fulfill the number cruncher. We were able to optimize their plan and make them comfortable with the direction and to ease previous tension caused by misunderstanding each other's thought processes.

Each learned to see how the other thought and to understand the reasons they each felt the way they did. There was not the usual judgment of right or wrong but just a feeling of "Wow, I never really knew that, and now I get it!" My job was to take this important information and develop a proper plan of action that would keep both on board happily, while finding ways that would help them accomplish their financial goals together. It truly wasn't just about the numbers, as the Rational first thought, but about having money harmony at home and accomplishing the couple's goals. There are a lot of ways to travel where you want to go, but choosing from the many paths and taking the path best for you and your family may take some outside-the-box considerations. You need to be comfortable with the strategy so that you can understand the reasons behind the decisions and stick to them.

To help you get a clearer picture of your own approach to financial management, take the test at the following link:

http://money.cnn.com/popups/2005/specials/money_type/
frameset.exclude.html

The test leverages the proven personality profile system called the Keirsey Temperament Sorter combined with a series of techniques that Statman and Wood developed to identify the various personality types. Each of the four personality types are explained in more detail at the end of the test.

*3. Put processes in place that help you better
manage your emotions—and your finances.*

Trying to manage your emotions in the moment, when they are at their strongest, usually does not work. Put a plan in place—in advance—that will allow you to manage your emotional reactions when you encounter a trigger.

Proactively set up systems such as:

- Automation
  Automate any goal and savings payments that may be vulnerable to emotional factors (such as retirement, vacations, and major purchases). Note that this strategy is not aimed at people who are having difficulty paying their bills, as it may result in bounced checks or cash shortfalls.

- Checks and balances
  Identify a trusted team of advisors with whom you consult on major financial decisions in order to balance overly emotional decisions. Never use a friend or spouse for major financial decisions. Although you may use a friend for smaller daily decisions, like identifying a colleague at work who

can remind you that you are limited to one mocha cappuccino per day, do not use a friend or colleague for financial decisions.

- Personal contract
  Write out a contract with yourself on how to deal with certain emotions in advance. For example, carefully outline how you will handle the continual frantic requests from your daughter when she calls from college asking for extra money.

4. Seek help.

Find a trusted wealth advisor or team leader to help you manage your emotions and conquer any dysfunctional behaviors. If you would rather manage your wealth without assistance, at the very least educate yourself on the common dysfunctional behaviors so that you can minimize their role in your personal finances—and in your life.

If emotional problems connected with money run very deep, seek counseling. Sometimes professional help is necessary to deal with deep-seated emotions related to traumatic experiences with financial issues. Complicating matters is the fact that financial issues are often closely intertwined with family issues. You may have been profoundly affected by a difficult experience with money in your childhood, in a difficult marriage, or in a business transaction. A professional counselor or therapist can become part of your team to help you with your wealth plan. In our wealth management practices, psychologists and other trained professionals are part of the team that we make available to clients.

The Next Steps

Money is a powerful tool—one that can spark a range of emotions such as joy, a sense of empowerment, and excitement. However, it can also spark debilitating emotions such as fear, anxiety, and frustration. Once you devise a strategy for enjoying your positive emotions and minimizing your negative ones, you are on your way to optimizing your wealth.

Now that you are more emotionally savvy, you are ready to start the journey laid out in the following chapters—toward enhancing, protecting, and sustaining your wealth.

CHAPTER THREE

Use an Integrative Approach

Integrate (verb)—to form, coordinate, or blend into a functioning or unified whole

As we learned in chapter 1, wealth is far more than the money that we have in our bank accounts. Rather, wealth encompasses all forms of resources, including financial, intellectual, social, emotional, and spiritual resources. Since wealth is broader than merely a financial statement, managing wealth demands a broader perspective.

Integrative wealth management is a unified, blended approach to helping you optimize your assets—and your quality of life. The approach integrates your financial plan, estate plan, and retirement plan into your personal vision and your wealth goals for you, your family, and your community. With integrative wealth management, you are able to make financial and life decisions consistent with your personal values and priorities.

With this more holistic approach to managing your wealth, you will be able to focus on issues that are far more important than merely managing an account balance, such as:

- Creating meaningful family, business, community, and artistic ventures

- Leaving an enduring legacy for family and community

- Building a life of significance and positive influence

If you use an integrative approach, you will build a powerful vision that is consistent with your personal values—and pursue your goals with passion, clarity, and focus. You will understand how your decisions fit into your overall vision. As a result, you will be more able to exercise discipline and pursue your goals with clarity and focus.

The Eight Dimensions of Wealth

Optimizing your wealth requires an integrative approach, so we must address *all* factors that can affect your family's wealth. To help us accomplish this goal, we use a special wealth optimization map called *Eight Dimensions of Wealth,* an eight-dimensional lens that allows us to see opportunities to enhance, protect, and sustain a family's wealth. It also provides our clients with a framework for making smart and thoughtful decisions about their wealth. A family's wealth can be positively or negatively impacted in all eight areas.

Each of the eight dimensions is an area of wealth management that you must address in order to achieve a truly integrative, unified management of all facets of your wealth. **Portfolio Management** is the management of your financial assets, including stocks, bonds, mutual funds, and other securities. Another crucial aspect of wealth management is **Asset Management** or the management of nonfinancial assets such as collectibles, business interests, and high-value items, such as aircraft. Optimizing both your portfolio and your nonfinancial assets requires careful **Tax Planning**, as well as long-term **Estate Planning** of how to distribute your assets to the next generation.

In order to ensure that you have an estate, you need to protect and sustain your wealth. A **Risk Management** plan allows you to carefully manage threats to your family's wealth. You also need a **Liability Management** plan in order to manage your liabilities such as mortgage and tuition payments.

Once you have carefully managed the first six dimensions of wealth, you are ready to engage in **Retirement Planning** to prepare for your retirement and in **Legacy Planning** to determine what assets you will leave for your heirs.

Next, we take an in-depth tour of each dimension to give you an idea of how to approach each aspect of wealth management. We also give you a glimpse of how we work with our clients.

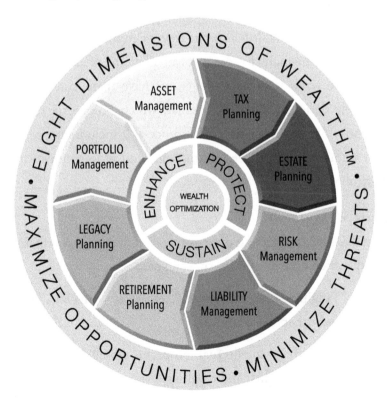

Portfolio Management

In Portfolio Management, the first of our Eight Dimensions of Wealth, we look at your financial assets. These include stocks, bonds, mutual funds, and other publicly traded securities. Portfolio Management is a critical dimension for most of our clients. While it does not always represent the largest concentration of wealth, it is more visible than other dimensions, because the prices of publicly traded assets are readily available in real time. Many of our clients also have significant balances in their retirement accounts consisting mainly of financial assets.

We consider *all* of your financial assets, regardless of where they are held. This includes taxable and tax-deferred accounts, such as corporate retirement plans, stock option programs, and individual retirement accounts.

Portfolio Management is one of the first dimensions we work on with new clients. It is also one that we monitor on an ongoing basis due to the many factors that can affect the financial markets. When we work with new clients, we have them complete our uniquely designed Planning Journal, which becomes a resource for the entire wealth management process. It includes useful tools that we use to analyze, design, manage, and monitor investment portfolios.

Asset Management

In the Asset Management dimension we look at your nonfinancial assets, which consist of three subcategories:

1. Tangible—art, collectibles, real estate, precious metals, and other "hard" assets

2. Intangible—intellectual property, closely held business interests, rights, and royalties

3. Special—private aircraft, yachts, and other high-value assets

When it comes to wealth optimization, nonfinancial assets can offer some attractive opportunities—and some formidable challenges. This is mainly due to unique characteristics of nonfinancial assets:

- They are less liquid than financial assets.

- They can be difficult to value.

- They can be difficult and expensive to insure.

- They can be difficult and expensive to buy and sell.

- Intangible assets can be completely overlooked.

- Special assets can present significant liability issues.

One of our key objectives in this dimension is to get you thinking about what you should be doing now and in the future with respect to these assets. For example, if you stand to inherit any nonfinancial assets, make sure you have recently appraised and adequately insured those assets. You should also make sure you have handled those assets in the most tax-efficient way possible.

Tax Planning

As we move into the third of our Eight Dimensions of Wealth, you will notice that the color at the top of the page in the Planning Journal changes from green to red. That is a subtle but important reminder that we are moving into a new quadrant of our map. In the first quadrant, we explored two dimensions, your financial and nonfinancial assets.

In the second quadrant, we explore the third and fourth dimensions—Tax Planning and Estate Planning. When it comes to wealth optimization, these two dimensions present unique challenges:

- Tax and estate planning issues tend to be complex.

- Tax and estate tax laws change frequently.

- Tax Planning is unique among the Eight Dimensions of Wealth in that it is directly affected by the decisions you make in the other seven dimensions. Virtually every decision you make has tax consequences.

- With the possible exception of accountants, IRS agents, and politicians, most people do not like to think about income taxes, much less talk about them.

- Even fewer like to think about estate taxes, which is understandable. Woody Allen summed up how many people feel when he said, "I am not afraid of death; I just don't want to be there when it happens."

For all of these reasons, the quality of advice you receive in the areas of tax and estate planning can have a significant impact on your family's wealth. So it is important to give these two dimensions the time and attention that you and your family deserve.

Estate Planning

Estate planning is one of the most difficult topics to address, because people want to avoid thinking about death. However, estate planning, or the process of organizing and preparing for the disposition of your assets upon your death, provides several key benefits:

1. It minimizes the administrative burdens and costs for your executor and heirs.

2. It minimizes estate and other taxes.

3. It maximizes the preservation of your assets and ensures that they are transferred in the manner that you choose.

There are countless examples of smart, successful people who died without having done the proper planning. Many passed away without wills or with wills that were out-of-date. Others left significant and unnecessary burdens for their heirs because they received poor advice or failed to be proactive when it came to estate planning.

The estate-planning field is littered with horror stories like these. To avoid your own horror story, thoughtfully craft your estate plan—and encourage your family members to carefully develop their own plans—with expert input.

Risk Management

As we move into the fifth of our Eight Dimensions of Wealth, the color at the top of the page changes from red to purple, indicating that we are moving into the quadrant focused on protecting wealth—in the dimensions of Risk Management and Liability Management. Risk comes in many forms and from many sources. To further complicate life, risk changes constantly, and new risks can emerge at any time. For all of these reasons, you should have a risk management plan that is reviewed on a regular basis.

Your plan should begin with a thorough assessment of all the major risks and other threats that can affect your family's wealth. This includes risks that exist currently as well as those that might exist in the future. Your plan should include strategies for managing those risks in the most cost- and tax-efficient way possible. Finally, your plan should include an annual review of all insurance policies that you and your family have in place.

Unfortunately, the concept of risk is one that few people want to discuss. However, ignoring risk or hoping that "bad things will never happen" is not a viable risk management strategy, especially if you want to optimize your wealth! The harsh reality is that risk management is an area where a single misstep or oversight can have a significant negative impact on your family's wealth.

Virtually every asset and every activity has a level of risk associated with it. Any family member can also get sick, get injured, or make a bad decision at any time. Clearly, the earlier that one adopts a risk management mindset the better.

Liability Management

In the next dimension, Liability Management, we look at your current and future liabilities. Current liabilities include mortgages, leases, personal loans, and other financial obligations

---

**THROUGH THE LENS OF EXPERIENCE:
*INSIGHTS ON WEALTH***

OPTIMIZE YOUR WEALTH:
To enhance one's wealth is to look for opportunity. If we're just speaking of monetary wealth, the answer is to look for needs in the community around you that have not been addressed.

I'm a big believer that there are, generally speaking, two kinds of people. First there's somebody who wants something and says, "I can't have that. I don't have the money" or "I can't have that. I don't have the requirements."

Then there's somebody who looks at the world and says, "I want that. How do I get that? What do I have to do to get that? Do I have to go to school? Do I have to learn how to fly? Do I have to join the military? Do I have to save my money? Do I have to get a second job?"

That is the characteristic that makes the second person wealthy, both in terms of money and in terms of other, more intangible forms of wealth.

—*Omar Ashmawy, entrepreneur*

that must be paid now. Future liabilities include financial obligations and large expenditures that will take place in the future. These include college tuitions, retirement income, and vacation homes.

There are three main ways to cover future liabilities:

- Save enough money to pay for them when they come due.

- Borrow the money when they come due.

- Sell assets to pay for the expenditures when they come due.

The concept of debt (in any form) has a negative connotation for some people. While we would never advocate taking on debt imprudently, there are situations in which borrowing money is in the best interest of your family's wealth. These are the types of conversations that we have and the types of decisions that you make when exploring this dimension of wealth.

Retirement Planning

As we move into the last quadrant, the color bar at the top of the page turns from purple to blue. The dimensions in this last quadrant, Retirement Planning and Legacy Planning, focus on sustaining wealth. The concept of retirement has different meanings for different people. For some, retirement is about working hard for a long time and then moving to a desirable location to enjoy their "golden years." For others, including many of our clients, the traditional concept of retirement is the furthest thing from their minds.

The term "lifestyle" is equally personal and subjective. Most of our clients lead active and productive lives well into their 70s,

80s, and even 90s. For them, retirement is more like a renaissance that involves starting new businesses and taking up encore careers. Many of our clients travel extensively during their renaissance years. Some take up art, writing, and other creative endeavors. Others become actively involved in their communities and with philanthropic activities.

To overcome these challenges and to accommodate every client's unique situation, at DreamCatcher Wealth Management, we integrated a more personalized approach called "personal renaissance planning". Our unique framework allows us to create a unique and meaningful plan for each of our clients. Personal renaissance planning looks at four interrelated areas:

HEALTH	We start with your health, because everything else depends on it. Our goal here is simply to understand how your health and that of relevant family members might affect your situation in the future.
ASPIRATIONS	We then challenge you to define your goals and objectives for your personal renaissance. What do you still want to achieve in life? Do you want to earn another degree? How about climb Mt. Kilimanjaro? We want you to have meaningful goals that will keep you motivated and allow you to keep having a positive impact.
LIFESTYLE	Next we guide you through a series of questions that explore the qualitative aspects of a renaissance-style life. Which leisure activities do you enjoy most? What is your ideal living environment? What are your passions when it comes to learning new things? Which causes and organizations do you support?

FINANCIAL	Based on what we learn in the first three areas, we can then help you make smart decisions about how to best use your assets and income sources. Our in-depth analysis addresses cash flow planning and retirement plan distribution strategies and helps you maximize any employee benefits. We can also help you plan for major transactions, such as the sale of your primary residence and the purchase of new assets.

Legacy Planning

To some, the word "legacy" conjures up visions of a university library or hospital wing that bears a family name like Morgan or Rockefeller. To others, the idea of leaving a legacy can be as simple—and meaningful—as documenting their family's genealogy in a way that celebrates and honors their ancestors. To us, the word legacy is synonymous with "gift". At its core, the dimension of Legacy Planning revolves around four fundamental questions:

1. *What* are you going to give?

2. *To whom* will you give it?

3. *When* are you going to give it to them?

4. *How* are you going to give it to them?

Spend some time thinking about these four fundamental questions. How do you really feel about these things, and what, whom, when, and how are you wanting your legacy to go? We will spend a great deal more detail on the Legacy Planning dimension in chapter 8.

With an integrative approach to wealth management, no area of your wealth is neglected. Managing your wealth according to a thoughtfully managed, integrative plan will ensure that you can meet your life goals and leave a legacy for your family and community. The beauty of integrative wealth management is that the legacy you leave for your family and community serves as the foundation for the portfolio of assets for the next generation, continuing the cycle of generational wealth building. The Legacy Planning phase of this generation becomes the Portfolio Management phase of the next one.

The next chapter starts you off on your journey of wealth optimization, which begins with checking your assumptions to ensure that you are operating on sound assumptions for optimizing your wealth.

CHAPTER FOUR

Check Your Assumptions

"It ain't what you don't know that gets you into trouble.
It's what you know that just ain't so."

—Mark Twain

Don't Believe Everything You
Hear, Read, or Believe

When it comes to your wealth, we agree that it's what you don't know *and* what you do know "that just ain't so" that gets you into trouble. In other words, *check your assumptions*. Much of what you assume to be true may not be.

When it comes to financial advice, *assume nothing*. Just because you like someone does not mean you are getting sound advice. When money is involved, trouble lurks everywhere and tends to rear its ugly head when you least expect it. This chapter provides you with the information you need for the challenging task of finding the right person to assist you in optimizing your wealth.

Staying Out of Trouble

If you want to optimize your wealth, the first thing to do is learn how to stay out of trouble. We recommend a three-step process:

1. **Make sure you understand the financial services playing field.**

   That includes learning about the various types of financial institutions and the financial advisors who work for them.

2. **Build a strong team.**

   Wealth management can be a complex process. You need a team approach to ensure that all aspects of your finances receive the expert attention they deserve. Make time to do your homework about the people who are giving you financial advice. Select individuals with the right fit—and then set up a system so that they can communicate with one another to create a truly integrative wealth management strategy that encompasses all of the Eight Dimensions of Wealth.

3. **Question the advice to ensure that it is truly in your best interest.**

   Regularly checking your assumptions—and the performance of your team—requires asking some tough questions of people with whom you may have worked for a long time.

Now we take an in-depth look at each step of the process:

Step 1: Make Sure You Understand the
Financial Services Playing Field

The financial services playing field is vast and can be a very confusing place to do business. For the purposes of this discussion, we focus on the retail segment of this enormous and important industry. The term "retail" is industry jargon and refers to companies that serve individual consumers and investors. The term "institutional" is used to describe nonindividual consumers and investors, such as endowments and foundations, insurance companies, money managers, mutual fund companies, and pension funds, to name a few. The one thing retail and institutional investors have in common is that, for the most part, they participate (buy and sell) in the same financial markets. An important difference lies in the fees that individual investors pay relative to their institutional counterparts. We talk more about the importance of fees shortly.

Step 2: Build a Strong Team

As we discussed in chapter 3, an integrative approach to wealth management involves coordinating and unifying the approaches to each of the Eight Dimensions of Wealth in order to achieve a cohesive, integrated overall strategy. Many of the various facets, or dimensions, of wealth require specialized expertise that can best be obtained through a team of expert financial advisors with a range of knowledge and experience.

As of 2014, there were approximately 300,000 financial advisors in the United States. According to the Financial Industry Regulatory Authority (FINRA), there are six basic groups of investment professionals:

- Financial planners
- Investment advisors

- Accountants

- Lawyers

- Insurance agents

- Brokers

The financial industry is largely self-regulating, with FINRA acting as the organization that establishes the rules, standards, and enforcement policies. FINRA offers a free database (http://www. finra.org/Investors/ToolsCalculators/BrokerCheck/) that you can use to investigate brokers, advisors, and other professionals. But be forewarned—even figuring out the different types of advisors and their titles can be an overwhelming task.

According to FINRA, there are over 150 titles in use today. As in any profession, the knowledge and experience among advisors varies greatly. This is why it is so important to do your due diligence before *and* after you hire someone. If you are working with a financial advisor today—regardless of how you met them—and you do *not* know the answers to the questions listed in this chapter, make an appointment to see your financial advisor as soon as possible. As the primary steward of your family's wealth, you owe it to yourself and your family to perform this due diligence. We address the concept of stewardship further in chapter 7.

TYPES OF FINANCIAL ADVISORS

ADVISOR	WHO THEY ARE	WHO REGULATES THEM	WHAT THEY OFFER
Broker	Person or company that buys and sells securities—stocks, bonds, mutual funds, and certain other investment products—on behalf of its customers (as broker), for its own account (as dealer), or both. Individuals who work for broker-dealers—the sales personnel whom most people call brokers—are technically known as registered representatives.	Broker-dealers must register with the Securities and Exchange Commission (SEC) and be members of FINRA. Individual registered representatives must register with FINRA, pass a qualifying examination, and be licensed by the state securities regulator.	Conduct financial transactions: buying or selling securities. Some provide investment research. Registered representatives can sell various products depending on the licenses (Series 6 or Series 7) that they hold.
Investment advisor (also known as asset manager, investment counselor, investment manager, portfolio manager, and wealth manager). Persons registered with an investment advisor firm are known as investment advisors or investment advisor representatives.	An investment advisor is a company that is paid for providing advice about securities to their clients. Not to be confused with financial advisor.	The SEC regulates investment advisors who manage $100 million or more in client assets. Advisors who manage less are regulated by state securities regulators.	Investment advisors provide investment advice and may manage investment portfolios or offer financial planning services. If properly licensed and registered with a broker, investment advisors may provide brokerage services (buying or selling investment products) or some combination of these services.

Financial planner	May be brokers, investment advisors, insurance agents, or practicing accountants—or they may have no financial credentials at all.	Some financial planners are not regulated by any specific body. Most, however, are regulated by the same bodies that regulate investment advisors.	Range of services varies widely. Some create a comprehensive plan, including investments, insurance, retirement, taxes, and estate planning. Others have a more limited scope. Important to understand scope of services before hiring.
Lawyer	Licensed to provide legal advice	State bar association	Legal advice, estate planning, tax law, and other services
Accountant	Professionals who assist individuals and companies with tax and financial planning, tax reporting, auditing, and management consulting	State board of accountancy	A CPA can help you consider the tax implications of financial decisions you make and assist with other tax-related issues, such as preparing annual tax returns. Some CPAs are also certified as a personal financial specialist (PFS), who can assist with financial planning and budgeting and may be registered with an investment advisor.
Insurance agent	Salespeople who can help individuals and companies obtain life, health, or property insurance policies and other insurance products	State insurance commission If an agent sells securities such as variable annuity policies, they must be licensed as a registered representative (securities salesperson).	May represent products of a single company or multiple companies. May sell securities.

Once you understand the financial services playing field, build your team—carefully. We recommend the following specialists for a well-balanced team:

- Investment advisor (wealth manager)

- Financial planner

- Accountant

- Lawyer (with the appropriate specialties: tax, estate, and so on)

- Insurance agent

- Broker

Don't allow just anyone to advise you on your finances. Money tends to attract "advisors" and friends of all types, some of them qualified and some not. So before you make a final decision on a financial professional, take these two steps:

1. Find out if the advisor's approach and skills align with your goals.

Seek out a professional with at least ten years of experience in financial advising. Check to see if your prospective advisor has expertise in the kinds of investments that are right for you. An advisor may have a niche specialty such as private placements, or investments in

THROUGH THE LENS OF EXPERIENCE:
INSIGHTS ON WEALTH

OPTIMIZE YOUR WEALTH:
What would you say are the keys to enhancing your wealth?

"I would say that it is what a lot of guys used to always tell me in the NFL but that I did not understand at first: The biggest thing is having a team and having people around you who can help you grow. So if you hit a plateau yourself, you have help.

Multiple brains are better than one, because you can't think of every-thing. If you do, somebody else can build on that because their mind works a little different than yours…

Everybody needs help along the way. I don't care who you are. You've got help at whatever stage you're at right now—you've got help from somebody. It's just a matter of building a team around you and having people that can help you grow."

—*Leigh Bodden, franchising entre-preneur and owner, Retro Fitness* startup ventures. However, knowledge of a single type of invest-ment vehicle will not enable you to build a strong diversified portfolio.

Other advisors specialize in high-growth, high-risk invest-ment strategies that may not match the level of risk you are willing to take. And some advisors simply may not be a fit for you and your work style. An interview will help you determine if the advisor's approach fits your goals and if the right chemistry exists between the two of you.

To set up your team, first be sure that each professional you hire is open to a team approach. Select a team leader, usually the financial planner or wealth manager, and determine if they already use a team approach. They may already have access to multiple experts in each field and also be willing to use experts you already have. The most important factor, however, is that the team leader is honest and places your interest above their own interest and their company's interest.

2. *Thoroughly understand costs.*

Understand exactly what services will be provided and for what cost. Like any professionals, financial advisors deserve to be compensated for their services. However, fees on top of standard compensation can severely limit returns—especially over the long timeframes involved in managing an investment portfolio. Carefully evaluate the compensation approaches. There are various compensation options to consider, including flat fee, hourly rate, and percentage of assets under management. Always ask for the compensation costs to be stated in several different ways so that you can compare and decide which one works best for you.

Here are the questions to ask a prospective advisor:

Knowledge and Experience

- How long have you been working as a financial advisor?

- What attracted you to the financial services industry?

- Where and when did you go to college, and what degrees do you hold?

- What experience do you have working with people who are like me?

- What licenses do you currently hold? Are you registered with a state, the SEC, or FINRA? If so, in what capacity?

- What relevant professional designations do you hold?

- Do you have any special areas of expertise?

- How long have you been with your current firm? Where did you work before?

- Are there any products or services you don't recommend? Why?

- Have you or your firm ever been disciplined by the SEC, FINRA, a state securities regulator, or another federal or state financial regulator?

- Have you ever had a professional license revoked?

- Have you ever been compensated by a new firm to change from one firm to another?

Business and Service Model

- Are you a registered representative?

- Are you registered as an investment advisor?

- Are you a fiduciary? How does your answer to this question affect me?

- What is your succession plan?

- Do you have a written business interruption plan?

- Where will my financial assets be held?

- What assurances do I have that my account and personal information will be secure?

Compensation Arrangements

- How much will I have to pay for your services? What is your usual hourly rate, flat fee, or commission?

- Are you compensated any other way for handling my account? If so, how? How much?

- Do you or your firm impose any minimum account balances? If so, what are they? And what happens if my portfolio falls below the minimum?

- How frequently will we meet to discuss my portfolio and the progress we are making toward my investment goals?

- Please explain all of the fees and commissions I am paying.

- Are you entitled to receive a bonus or an incentive for selling any particular investment products or services of any kind?

- How many firms have you worked for? If more than one, how long did you work at each firm, and why did you move? (Many financial advisors, especially those working for brokerage firms, get paid large "recruiting bonuses" to move from one company to another every few years. Multiple shifts to various companies can create instability for you as the client.)

Step 3: Check Your Assumptions and Monitor Performance

Monitoring your advisors' performance is crucial for ensuring that the performance of your portfolio matches your goals. Once you have set goals, establish a system of reporting. Be sure that you understand whether fees are included or not included in the standard reporting of returns. And be sure to *compare returns to goals*. Earning 6 percent may sound phenomenal—unless the goal was 8!

Take these steps to effectively monitor performance:

- Find a benchmark portfolio against which you can compare your portfolio's performance.

- Read, read, read! Stay up-to-date on market trends.

THROUGH THE LENS OF EXPERIENCE: *INSIGHTS ON WEALTH*

OPTIMIZE YOUR WEALTH:
When it comes to defining the benefits that I get from my advisors, it's hard to explain any single one or two things. I depend on a group of advisors, both for my personal life and my business. To me, the benefits from my advisors are in the base of knowledge that they have on how to preserve and protect what I have accumulated and for planning for the future. They know vehicles and mechanisms and trusts and things like that that can allow me to achieve the goals that I could not and did not know of myself. So it's the knowledge that they have.

—*Christopher Moeller, MD, founder, Moeller Dermatology*

- Be sure that your team leader is staying on top of your team to ensure that you are achieving your goals with a risk level that is consistent with the plan that you originally devised.

- Communication is key! If you have any questions or changes in your situation, bring it to the attention of the team immediately.

- Be sure that your team communicates any relevant market changes or other changes to you in a timely manner.

By building the right team—and then monitoring that team and checking your assumptions on an ongoing basis, you can avoid having knowledge "that just ain't so."

CHAPTER FIVE

Keep an Eye on the Future

> *"Life is divided into three terms—that which was, that which is and that which will be. Let us learn from the past to profit by the present and from the present to live better in the future."*

—William Wordsworth

How many times have you or someone you know said, "If I only knew then what I know now"? Obviously, you can't change your past, but you can profoundly influence *someone's future*. Many people do not realize that the major events (and even some minor ones) that take place throughout our lives are more predictable than we might think—for this reason, I encourage all of my clients to *keep an eye on the future*. Notice I did not say *your* future. When we talk about "the future" we are talking about multiple *futures*, the futures of all family members who stand to benefit from—or impact—your wealth.

This chapter introduces you to the concept of life stage planning as a tool to help you understand your stage of life. Most importantly, the tool helps you understand the health-related, financial, emotional, spiritual, and relationship assets and liabilities of each stage:

- Where you have been in life

- Where you are now

- Where you are going

Understanding the resource requirements of these life stages tells you what quality of physical, spiritual, emotional, and intellectual life you and your family can support, now and in the future. This chapter introduces the life stages and then provides some questions to help you set goals that fit your life stage.

Life Stage Planning

It is said that the ancient Greeks viewed human life as unfolding in a series of seven-year stages. This general concept can be a very useful tool in predicting, or at least anticipating, future events.

The Human Odyssey

Psychologist Thomas Armstrong offers a philosophical version of a life stage model. In his book *The Human Odyssey: Navigating the Twelve Stages of Life*, Armstrong writes, "Each stage of life has its own unique *gift* to contribute to the world. We need to value each one of these gifts if we are to truly support the deepest needs of human life."[1]

Listed below are Armstrong's 12 stages (and the corresponding "gifts") of the human life cycle:

1. Prebirth: Potential

2. Birth: Hope

3. Infancy (Ages 0–3): Vitality

4. Early childhood (Ages 3–6): Playfulness

5. Middle childhood (Ages 6–8): Imagination

6. Late childhood (Ages 9–11): Ingenuity

7. Adolescence (Ages 12–20): Passion

8. Early adulthood (Ages 20–35): Enterprise

9. Midlife (Ages 35–50): Contemplation

10. Mature adulthood (Ages 50–80): Benevolence

11. Late adulthood (Age 80+): Wisdom

12. Death and dying: Life

The first three cycles—prebirth, birth, and infancy—represent the child's potential, the hope and optimism the child spreads as it enters the world, and the vitality and unrelenting energy of infancy.

During the next four cycles—early childhood through adolescence—children create their own worlds through play as they innovate with their endless imaginations. The older they get, the more aware they become of their surroundings, and their imaginations sharpen to provide inspiration for everything they do, from arts to science. By the time they are in late childhood and adolescence, they have a wide range of social skills and strategies to deal with the world in place—just in time for puberty to unleash their passion for life and the changes it may bring.

In the stages of adulthood, Armstrong says, early adults begin to take responsibility for the life they are building. At midlife, ages 35–50, adults often begin to reflect on the past and then move forward with new understanding. In mature adulthood, ages 50–80, they become society's volunteers, mentors, and philanthropists as they share their benevolence with greater society. Late adulthood, as you would expect, is focused on sharing the wisdom acquired over the years and passing it down in an effort to help others.

Armstrong's final stage, death and dying, is focused on life—learning about its value and how to live it to the fullest.

For me, these 12 steps of life provide a philosophical approach to looking for outside-the-box ideas at every stage of our lives. For years, I have said, "I hope to always be able to see life through the eyes of a four-year-old." To a young child, there is only wonder, everything is new, and the favorite question is *why?* Being able to harness this mindset helped me write this book and helps me when I work with clients. When it comes to finances, the *why* for most people changes with time, so I never stop asking. I learn so much that way about my clients and their family dynamics, which ultimately helps me to offer better recommendations to optimize their wealth.

In addition to helping to anticipate future events, these life stages offer an encouraging way to contemplate our legacies: what we intend to leave behind in the hearts and minds of the people we care about. As you may recall from our wealth optimization map in chapter 3, Legacy Planning is one of the Eight Dimensions of Wealth that we address as part of our integrative approach to working with clients. We can start working on our legacy, in our everyday lives, much earlier than many of us think. As Armstrong so eloquently states:

> *"Since each stage of life has its own unique gift*
> *to give to humanity, we need to do whatever we*
> *can to support each stage and to protect each*
> *stage from attempts to suppress its individual*
> *contribution to the human life cycle.*

Thus, we need to be wary, for example, of attempts
to thwart a young child's need to play through
the establishment high-pressure formal academic
preschools. We should protect the wisdom of
aged from elder abuse. We need to do what we
can to help our adolescents at risk. We need to
advocate for prenatal education and services
for poor mothers and support safe and healthy
birthing methods in third world countries.

We ought to take the same attitude toward
nurturing the human life cycle as we do toward
saving the environment from global warming
and industrial pollutants. For by supporting
each stage of the human life cycle, we will help
to ensure that all of its members are given care
and helped to blossom to their fullest degree."[2]

Back to the Future

A more practical approach to life stage planning is provided by renowned futurist and author Verne Wheelwright in his book *It's Your Future: Make It a Good One.*[3] Wheelwright's model contains ten stages of life, although the last two are health related and do not come into play for all individuals. Perhaps even more important than the stages themselves are the transitional periods *between* the stages, which are often the most difficult.

WHEELWRIGHT MODEL

LIFE STAGE	CHARACTERISTICS OF LIFE STAGE
Infant	Birth through two years. Dependent, brain developing, learning motor skills and sensory abilities.
Child	3–9 years. Growing and mastering motor skills and language. Learning to play and socialize. Continued growth, formal school, and organized activities.
Adolescent	10–19 years. Growth spurts. Puberty brings hormonal changes and reactions. Strong emotions may rule decisions. Behavioral risks.
Young adult	20–29 years. Completing education and beginning career and family. Potential coping and financial pressures.
Adult	30–39 years. Managing family and career growth. Increasing numbers of couples start families in this stage. Continued coping pressures.
Middle age	40–60 years. First signs of aging and effects of lifestyle: menopause, children are leaving the nest, grandchildren arrive, career peak. Aging parents may require care.
Independent elder	Age 60 onward. More signs of aging and lifestyle effects. Eligible for government-provided retirement and health-care benefits or private pensions. Retirement, discretionary time. Some health problems and medications. May care for others.
Vulnerable elder	Optional stage. Beginning of frailty, cognitive difficulties, or multiple health problems. Require some assistance. Not able to drive. Possible move to assisted living.
Dependent elder	Optional stage. Requires daily care. Unable to perform all personal functions. Possible move to a nursing home.

Some people prefer the more direct approach of this model, which I often use as a reference for clients as they start to consider legacy planning and think about higher-impact life events. Some prefer different perspectives when it comes to looking at their future and their past in the different life cycles, so finding the approach you feel fits you best is another insight into how best to develop and optimize your wealth plan.

The key to planning for the future lies in anticipating which events are likely to occur at each stage—and planning accordingly. To help with planning, Wheelwright provides a useful list of both common events and less typical "high-impact" events.

LIFE STAGE	COMMON EVENTS	HIGH-IMPACT EVENTS
Infant	Learning, walk, talk Minor illnesses	Serious illness
Child	School Growth Minor injuries and illnesses	Serious illness Bullying Parents divorce
Adolescent	Complete required schooling Puberty, emotions, sex Physical growth Begin driving Risky behaviors	Accidents, serious injuries Arrest Pregnancy Parents divorce Death of parent or friend
Young adult	Complete higher education Begin career Move to own housing Marriage First child	Accidents Illness or injury of child Job loss
Adult	Career pressures/advances Managing family Last child	Financial pressures Divorce Job loss
Middle age	Menopause-end child bearing Aging sings Empty nest Grandchildren Parents retire Peak earnings/savings	Serious or chronic illness, self or spouse Parent illness or death Crime victim Job loss Divorce
Independent elder	Eligible for retirement Social Security, Medicare (US) Work/retirement choices Discretionary time Great grandchildren Increased aging signs Relocate, new friends Travel Problems in children's lives	Retirement Changing roles & social Serious illness, self or spouse Death of spouse Become caregiver Stop driving

Vulnerable elder	Frailty Cognitive problems Risk of falls Risk of scams, victim of crime	Falls, injuries Assisted living
Dependent elder	Reduced activities Increased medical Reduced social	Dependant on others Losing control of life Nursing home
End of life	Reduced activities and social Increased medical Good-byes	Terminal diagnosis Hospice

We should always be thinking about our current stage of life and the stages to come. Although we cannot see life in advance, we can try to anticipate our stages in order to optimize the opportunities and minimize the risks. It can really be a great place to stop and look at where you are now and the changes that may happen as you age. If you are planning something in the future, imagining what stage you or your heir may be in at that future point may bring better clarity or possibilities than first thought. This visualization can really help you better see options for enhancing or protecting your wealth during that specific stage. I have seen this technique give a few aha moments when a client realizes a new possible outcome and says, "I would have never thought about it that way, but now I see why we are talking about future possibilities."

Many risks may be well into the future, but we must still consider them now in our risk management and legacy plans. At times, it can be uncomfortable to think about the later stages of life, but by looking at the whole picture, you can have a comprehensive plan that flows through your entire life—not just unconnected pieces. Learning about my clients' perspectives on life helps me lead them through the journey of optimizing their options.

Once you have your own life stages planned, you then need to consider the life stages of those who will either influence or inherit your wealth. Chapter 6 serves as your guide to "getting your family involved."

To help you set goals that address both the common and high-impact events of each life stage, the next chapter provides thought-provoking questions and exercises.

---

[1] Armstrong, R. (2008), *The Human Odyssey: Navigating the Twelve Stages of Life*. New York: Sterling.

[2] Ibid.

[3] Wheelwright, V. (2012), *It's Your Future: Make It a Good One*. Harlinger, TX: Personal Futures Network.

CHAPTER SIX

Get Your Family Involved

"In every conceivable manner, the family is link to our past, bridge to our future."

—Alex Haley, *Roots*

Ah, the family. The family is where we can most be ourselves. However, many people feel uncomfortable discussing financial matters with members of their own family. If that is the case in your family, I encourage you to be the person who "steps up to the plate" to change things. In most cases, it is in everyone's financial best interest to participate in periodic conversations about the family's wealth. You can do this without getting into specifics or sensitive details. You should

THROUGH THE LENS OF WEALTH: *INSIGHTS FROM WEALTHY INDIVIDUALS*

OPTIMIZE YOUR WEALTH:
What did you learn as a child from your family that helped you when it came to building wealth for you and your family?

"My great-grandfather started the first Chevrolet dealership here in the Washington/Maryland area. It went from one dealership in 1940 to 15 dealerships in 2009. He instilled a work value in his grandsons—including my father—who grew up without parents and were raised by their grandparents.

continued on next page.

continued from previous page.

You have to work hard. You have to work hard, you have to build relationships, and you have to respect others. It's the only way that you're going to be able to build your own capability and wealth, and ultimately, to continue that wealth.

My dad never had to go to work every single day, because there were already finances in place where he really didn't have to work. But he worked his rear end off, probably to prove himself to some degree to his grandfather but mostly to show my brother and I what it takes to maintain and generate more wealth for yourself."

—*Molly Dworken Herman, entrepreneur*

also be actively learning about those you are thinking of making your heirs.

In chapter 5, we introduced the concept of life stage planning. Understanding life stages is vital to achieving our three-fold mission of enhancing, protecting, and sustaining wealth. Knowing your current life stage—and more importantly, the life stage that is coming next—will enable you to optimize your wealth.

Why is having an understanding of life stages so important? It's because there are some fairly predictable events that take place at each of the various stages. Each of those events is associated with certain financial needs or objectives. The sooner you recognize both the events and the related financial need, the sooner you can incorporate these insights into your planning.

For all these reasons, we encourage you to carefully consider all of your family members as you work on your Planning Journal. There are three key steps to involving your family in your wealth management process:

1. Determine whom to include in your wealth management planning and conversations.

2. Determine family members' life stages.

3. Determine the role that relevant family members play in optimizing your wealth.

To assist you, we provide you with a graphical worksheet below that shows:

- Which stage each of your family members are in today

- Which stages they will be entering in the future

- What role they play in your wealth management planning

Family Planning Worksheets

YOU AND YOUR DESCENDANTS			
Name	Birth Year	Name	Birth Year
Your Name		Spouse's Name	
YOUR CHILDREN			
Name	Birth Year	Name	Birth Year
•		•	
•		•	
•		•	
YOUR GRANDCHILDREN			
Name	Birth Year	Name	Birth Year
•		•	
•		•	
•		•	
•		•	
•		•	

-
-
-
-

NONFAMILY MEMBERS

Name	Birth Year	Name	Birth Year
•		•	
•		•	
•		•	
•		•	
•		•	
•		•	

YOUR FAMILY   SPOUSE'S FAMILY

YOUR PARENTS

Name	Birth Year	Name	Birth Year
•		•	
•		•	
•		•	
•		•	

YOUR GRANDPARENTS

Name	Birth Year	Name	Birth Year
•		•	
•		•	
•		•	
•		•	

YOUR SIBLINGS

Name	Birth Year	Name	Birth Year

Name	Birth Year	Name	Birth Year
•		•	
•		•	
•		•	
•		•	
•		•	
•		•	
•		•	
•		•	

OTHER FAMILY MEMBERS

Name	Birth Year	Name	Birth Year
•		•	
•		•	
•		•	
•		•	
•		•	
•		•	

Now list each person, their life stage, and the role that they play in your wealth management planning:

YOU AND YOUR DESCENDANTS

Family Member	Life Stage	Role
Children		
Grandchildren		

Other family
members

Nonfamily members

YOU AND YOUR FAMILY

Family Member	Life Stage	Role
Parents		
Grandparents		

Siblings

Other family
members

Nonfamily members

YOUR SPOUSE'S FAMILY

Family Member	Life Stage	Role
Parents		
Grandparents		

Siblings

Other family members

Nonfamily members

This will give you an idea of where you should start in building the life stage planning chart and which heirs to include in the process. Planning can get very complicated as you expand your list, which is why a team may be needed to help with the various options you find after doing this exercise. Important questions to ask are:

- Will this help me optimize all of my options and recognize the risks and opportunities of each choice?

- Why would I include this person to handle these assets or duties?

- Why would I exclude this person from handling these assets or duties?

The Roles of Family Members

Family members play many different roles in wealth management planning. Here are some of the primary roles they may play:

1. **Heir**

   An inheritor is poised to inherit your wealth. You will need to evaluate an heir's ability to responsibly manage and carry on your legacy. Key questions to ask are:

   - What is the heir's moral character?

   - What is the heir's financial literacy?

   - How do they handle emotionally, intellectually, socially, or financially challenging situations?

   - What is the heir's current financial situation?

   - Will the inheritance completely transform their financial situation?

   - What training is necessary to prepare the heir to manage the wealth?

   - Are your heirs competent to inherit your wealth, or will they just quickly spend the money on expensive gifts?

You may want to set up some financial education to equip your heirs to better manage your hard-earned assets. More and more people today give their heirs instruction in financial management fundamentals. They also get heirs involved in wealth management at an earlier age so that the heirs hone their skills in managing and monitoring financial assets. Many wealthy people also actively seek to learn about the moral character and values of their heirs in different situations before leaving them substantial assets.

THROUGH THE LENS OF EXPERIENCE: *INSIGHTS ON WEALTH*

OPTIMIZE YOUR WEALTH:
When it comes to training kids how to balance their checkbooks, we absolutely need that because kids now have access to everything. They see everything on TV. Everybody lives well. They see it on the Internet—all these wonderful things that you could buy and do—and they want it all. But they have to learn that even though the world is their oyster and theirs for the taking, they have to be able to budget well. They need to know how to invest, and they need to be able to manage their own sometimes insatiable desires.

—Lisa Spoden, health-care entrepreneur

2. Builder

Builders do more than merely inherit. Rather, they play an active role in managing or building the assets. They have the potential to build your assets and take your wealth to the next level—or not.

As an example, builders may be individuals who are in a position to decide to run the family business. If they choose to run the business, they play a pivotal role in shaping your legacy.

In addition to the issues that must be evaluated for an heir, discussed above, the following questions are necessary to evaluate a builder's ability to positively impact your legacy:

- Is the builder interested in building?

- What skills, qualities, and experience does the builder have that are necessary to build your assets?

- What skills, qualities, and experience does the builder lack that are necessary to build your assets?

  □ Academic knowledge

  □ Work experience

  □ Personal network

  □ Financial capital

  □ Money personality

  □ Ethics

  □ Age

  □ Ability to lead

- What barriers exist that could limit the builder's success?

  □ Health issues

  □ Unsupportive spouse or family members

  □ Competing goals

3. **Family Member Leaving Wealth**

   Another role that a family member may play is to leave an inheritance to you or others in your family. Key questions to ask and issues to evaluate are:

- What is the nature of the inheritance?

- When do you anticipate receiving it?

- Are there any obligations or requirements attached to the inheritance?

- Are others involved in the inheritance?

- How well have you prepared them to receive this inheritance?

  Although these questions are not always easy to ask, they will help you to prepare to optimize your wealth by effectively integrating your family into wealth management—for a truly integrative process.

As wealth managers, we lead our clients and relevant family members in their journey of wealth management and optimization. We help them ask—and answer—the hard questions. Even if you do not have a qualified wealth advisor to guide you, you can probe the topic areas presented in this chapter so that both you and your family are at least somewhat prepared. When you do find the right wealth advisors to help you build your team, you will have a great foundation.

CHAPTER SEVEN

Strive for Stewardship

"Do not save what is left after spending, but spend what is left after saving. If you buy things you do not need, soon you will have to sell the things you need."

—Warren Buffet

Stewardship is an ethic that embodies responsible planning and management of valuable resources. The concept of stewardship is closely linked to sustainability. Responsible stewards plan ahead to ensure that their family's wealth is preserved, or sustained, from one generation to the next.

When it comes to generational wealth, effective stewards make prudent decisions on behalf of all family members. Listed below are some suggestions that will help you sustain your family's generational wealth:

1. **Make time to understand the environment.**
   There are many factors that can affect your family's wealth in a positive or negative way. We will make sure that you and your family have the information you need to make prudent decisions.

2. **Find a wealth advisor who can serve as a true partner in optimizing your wealth.**

The financial landscape is complex and ever changing. You need the knowledge and insights of an expert.

3. **Be proactive.**

In order to maximize opportunities and minimize risks, you must seek them out and act on them. Truly optimizing and maximizing your wealth demands far more than passive management to protect your assets. Rather, it requires active management to realize the upside, protect from the downside, initiate new ventures, and exit ventures that do not make sense. That is why I use the Planning Journal to gather detailed information to develop a unique optimized plan for my wealth clients.

4. **Be flexible.**

The environment is constantly changing, and the rate of change is accelerating. Be willing to make moves with your portfolio that allow you

THROUGH THE LENS OF EXPERIENCE:
INSIGHTS ON WEALTH

OPTIMIZE YOUR WEALTH:
What principles of financial stewardship have you learned that have helped you when it comes to building—and sustaining—wealth for you and your family?

"I was raised by a single mother, and a couple things my mother always told me were, number one: 'Chris, you've got to learn how to take care of yourself, because there probably isn't going to be somebody to take care of you.'

Number two was when I was in college, and first getting out on my own financially, she advised me: 'Always pay your bills first, and what you got left over, you can use for play or things like that.'

continued on next page.

to capitalize on these changes—and avoid being damaged by them.

5. **Consider everyone who has a vested interest in your wealth.**
    This includes your heirs as well as any organizations you plan to support financially. As we discussed in chapter 5, it is crucial to thoroughly understand who plays a role in your wealth—and to equip them with the tools they need to optimize and sustain it into the future.

continued from previous page.

One of the bills...she always considered bills...was savings, so I do that to this day. Before I ever take any money from my business for my own personal use, I not only make sure that I've paid all of the business expenses but also that I've maximized my retirement and my savings. I do that first, and if I don't have any money left over, I don't take any money home.

I still live that way."

—Christopher Moeller, MD, founder, Moeller Dermatology

6. **Learn as much as you can about the financial affairs of your relatives and anyone else from whom you stand to inherit assets.**
    Understand the fundamentals of the financial affairs of anyone who will bequeath assets to you.

    *   What is the timing of the inheritance?

    *   What assets are involved?

    *   Are there any risks inherent in the relative's financial situation that could jeopardize the inheritance?

    *   Is there any role that they can play now to optimize the assets?

7. **Begin to build your knowledge of valuable illiquid assets.** Assets such as art, business interests, and real property require more specialized management techniques and expertise.

8. **Involve every family member who has or will have decision-making responsibilities.** Once you understand the financial literacy and competency of each of your family members, educate and equip them as needed, as described in chapter 5.

9. **Evaluate the quality of advice and service you are receiving on a regular basis.** This includes accountants, attorneys, physicians, and other service providers—anyone whose advice can affect your wealth. You should do this at least annually.

10. **Be an advocate for your family and friends when it comes to their financial affairs. Do not assume anything!** A common and very costly mistake is assuming that your parents or other family members have done the proper estate planning or that their documents are up-to-date. Again, be proactive about this. Do not assume that family members are receiving the best advice or service. I have seen countless estates go awry because of poor planning. The person leaving the inheritance does not know the misery that is often left behind. With these principles of personal and family financial stewardship in action, you are positioned to better live the life that you want to live and leave the legacy that you desire to leave.

Avoid becoming a statistic! Ensure that your business or legacy lasts into the third generation. Remember, the easy way to ensure that your legacy does *not* endure is to leave the inheritance to a group of uneducated heirs all at once.

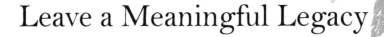

CHAPTER EIGHT

Leave a Meaningful Legacy

"Outlive your life!"
—*Max Lucado*

You may or may not be thinking of leaving a hospital wing in your name—it is all about what *you* want to do. But if you remember from chapter 3, we talked about how it may all come together. I hope you spent some time contemplating a few, if not all, of the four fundamental questions below. Now, let's talk more in depth about these questions and how they fit into your dynamic legacy planning strategies.

As we said earlier, to us, the word *legacy* is synonymous with *gift*. At its core, the Legacy Planning dimension involves four fundamental questions:

1. *What* are you going to give?

2. *Who* will receive it?

3. *When* are you going to give it to them?

4. *How* are you going to give it to them?

As you contemplate your legacy, be sure to include both tangible and intangible gifts. Your tangible gifts are relatively easy to identify. They include both financial and nonfinancial assets. Most of your tangible gifts will be transferred to your heirs in accordance with your estate planning documents.

Your intangible gifts include your knowledge, your values, and the time you spend with the people who care most about you. In most cases, intangible gifts do not have a monetary value, yet they are often more cherished than their tangible counterparts. In addition, they are typically given to their recipients while the donor is living. A wise person once said that the most valuable gift you can give to the people who care most about you is simply to take better care of yourself so you can spend more time with them.

To that end, we developed a planning tool that will help you identify your intangible gifts. Our Personal Legacy Journal has seven worksheets. Each worksheet has a series of questions that will get you

THROUGH THE LENS OF EXPERIENCE:
INSIGHTS ON WEALTH

OPTIMIZE YOUR WEALTH:
What qualities do you look for in a wealth advisor when it comes to building—and sustaining—wealth for you and your family?

"Empathy comes to mind, but that's not exactly it. It's an ability for an advisor to put themself in my shoes and do what's right for me—not only at this point in time but also in looking at my situation and forecasting what I'm going to need, financially and spiritually. It's meeting me where I'm at and helping me to forecast forward where I need to be in my spiritual growth, in my financial growth, or in whatever area.

It's not just to meet me where I'm at but to help me interpret what my needs are. That's not my area of expertise, so a good advisor in any of these areas…needs to be able to interpret what I am saying and help me get there."

—Lisa Spoden, health-care entrepreneur

thinking at a deeper, more meaningful level about your life in the following "legacy domains":

- Your health
- Your knowledge
- Your family values
- Your relationships
- Your community
- The world at large
- Your financial legacy

Legacy Domain #1: Health

How important do you consider your health to be at this stage of your life? 10 = most important	1	2	3	4	5	6	7	8	9	10
How satisfied are you with your health today? 10 = most satisfied	1	2	3	4	5	6	7	8	9	10

In order of priority, list up to ten things you can do to maximize your longevity (the more specific, the better).

1.	6.
2.	7.
3.	8.
4.	9.
5	10.

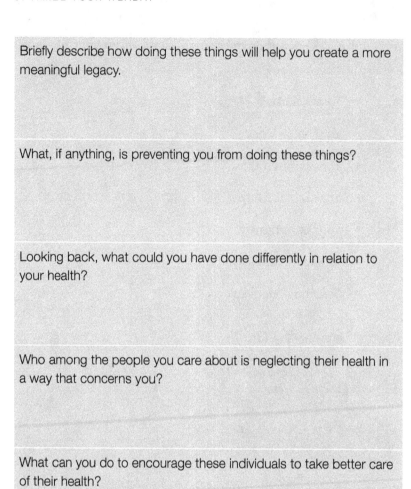

Briefly describe how doing these things will help you create a more meaningful legacy.

What, if anything, is preventing you from doing these things?

Looking back, what could you have done differently in relation to your health?

Who among the people you care about is neglecting their health in a way that concerns you?

What can you do to encourage these individuals to take better care of their health?

No matter how you answered the question about the importance of your health, your response should have been a 10 on a scale of 1 to 10. Your physical, spiritual, and mental health provides the foundation for any legacy that you are building. Be honest about areas of improvement in your habits, diet, and both mental and physical exercise.

Whether you are healthy or are in poor or failing health, consult trusted health advisors to develop a plan to make positive changes. Enlist the help of friends and family. Many people, when faced with a health crisis, are motivated to make meaningful life changes that can extend or enhance their lives.

Legacy Domain #2: Your Knowledge

How important do you consider knowledge acquisition to be in a person's life?	1	2	3	4	5	6	7	8	9	10
How satisfied are you with your level of education and knowledge today?	1	2	3	4	5	6	7	8	9	10

In order of priority, list up to ten professional subjects that you consider to be your areas of expertise. If you are retired, indicate if they are still marketable (Y/N).			In order of priority, list up to ten personal subjects (hobbies or personal interest) that you consider to be your areas of expertise. Indicate if they are marketable (Y/N).		
1.	Y	N	1.	Y	N
2.	Y	N	2.	Y	N
3.	Y	N	3.	Y	N
4.	Y	N	4.	Y	N
5.	Y	N	5.	Y	N
6.	Y	N	6.	Y	N
7.	Y	N	7.	Y	N
8	Y	N	8	Y	N
9.	Y	N	9.	Y	N
10.	Y	N	10.	Y	N

To the extent that it is marketable or transferrable, who would benefit from having access to your knowledge and expertise? Attach a separate sheet if necessary.

Family and friends	For-profit organizations and other entities that would be willing to pay you for your expertise	Nonprofit organizations and other entities with whom you would share your expertise on a pro bono basis
•	•	•
•	•	•
•	•	•
•	•	•
•	•	•
•	•	•
•	•	•
•	•	•

Briefly describe how you can use your knowledge and expertise to create a more meaningful legacy.

If you were so inclined, how could you monetize (make money from) your expertise?

Looking back, what could you have done differently in your own knowledge development?

Who among the people you care about is neglecting their knowledge development in a way that concerns you?

What can you do to encourage these individuals to optimize this dimension of *their* legacy?

Knowledge is one of the most underutilized assets. Rarely do we take inventory of our knowledge. Now that you have honestly assessed your knowledge resources, determine how to use it. Your knowledge may be the foundation of a business idea or the seed of a new strategy to transform the mission of a nonprofit organization. Determine where it should be shared—and begin sharing it!

Legacy Domain #3: Your Family Values

How important is it to you that your family's history and values be preserved for future generations?	1	2	3	4	5	6	7	8	9	10
How satisfied are you with the effort you have made to preserve your family's history and values?	1	2	3	4	5	6	7	8	9	10

In order of priority, list up to ten facts or stories about your family that are worthy of sharing and preserving. Use headings for now. Have these been documented (Y/N)?			In order of priority, list up to ten family values and guiding principles that you feel should be shared and preserved. Have these been codified or documented (Y/N)?		
1.	Y	N	1.	Y	N
2.	Y	N	2.	Y	N
3.	Y	N	3.	Y	N
4.	Y	N	4.	Y	N
5.	Y	N	5.	Y	N
6.	Y	N	6.	Y	N
7.	Y	N	7.	Y	N
8	Y	N	8	Y	N
9.	Y	N	9.	Y	N
10.	Y	N	10.	Y	N

Briefly describe how preserving and sharing your family's history and values can help you create a more meaningful legacy.

Looking back, what could you have done differently in preserving and sharing your family's history and values?

Who among the people you care about is neglecting their family history and values in a way that concerns you?

What can you do to encourage these individuals to optimize this dimension of their legacy?

A family's history and values are its most treasured assets. However, they are often unspoken rather than spoken—and rarely recorded. Yet they have the power to change individuals, families, organizations, and communities. Knowing that Great-Great-Granddad built an enterprise after fleeing the Nazis can spark a renewed entrepreneurial vision. Knowing that historical records showed that a host of your ancestors defied the shackles of slavery to learn to read and write can fuel a passion for education. Knowing how anticipated and celebrated her birth was can nurture a granddaughter's budding self-esteem.

Discover, tell, and document your family history and values!

Legacy Domain #4: Your Relationships

When it comes to your personal legacy, how important is the quality of your relationships to you?	1	2	3	4	5	6	7	8	9	10
How satisfied are you with the overall quality of your relationships?	1	2	3	4	5	6	7	8	9	10
How satisfied are you with the effort you have put into your relationships up to this this point in your life?	1	2	3	4	5	6	7	8	9	10

Use the box to the right of each name entered below to indicate the state of your relationship with that individual today. 10 = optimal state

Your ten closest family members		Your ten closest friends		Your ten most important business relationships	
1.		1.		1.	
2.		2.		2.	
3.		3.		3.	
4.		4.		4.	
5.		5.		5.	
6.		6.		6.	
7.		7.		7.	
8		8		8	
9.		9.		9.	
10.		10.		10.	

Briefly describe how doing everything you can to optimize your relationships with others can help you create a more meaningful legacy.

Who among the people you care about is neglecting their relationships in a way that concerns you?

What can you do to encourage these individuals to build and nurture healthier relationships?

Relationships are among the most important aspects of a person's legacy. However, assessing your relationships and their legacy impact can be one of the most challenging tasks in legacy planning. Ask yourself if your relationships are in need of greater communication, forgiveness, or reconciliation. Are there relationships that you are neglecting? Are there some that warrant more time—or simply—more care?

Examine your relationships closely and begin to take the steps to leave the legacy not merely on financial statements but on hearts.

THROUGH THE LENS OF EXPERIENCE: *INSIGHTS ON WEALTH*

OPTIMIZE YOUR WEALTH:
Wealth is not just what you have in your bank account but also what you give back to society in general, however you define what you want to do philanthropy-wise... Wealth is not just your finances but also your day-to-day interactions. It's how you treat yourself and others, which stands apart from corporate philanthropy or personal philanthropy.

—*Molly Dworken Herman, Entrepreneur*

Legacy Domain #5: Your Community

How important is the quality of life in your community to you?	1	2	3	4	5	6	7	8	9	10
How satisfied are you with the quality of life in your community?	1	2	3	4	5	6	7	8	9	10
How satisfied are you with your personal efforts to enhance the quality of life in your community?	1	2	3	4	5	6	7	8	9	10

In order of priority, list up to ten things you can do to improve the quality of life in your community.

1.	6.
2.	7.
3.	8
4.	9.
5.	10.

Briefly describe how enhancing the quality of life in your community can help you create a more meaningful legacy.

Looking back, what could you have done differently in relation to the quality of life in your community?

Who among the people you care about is neglecting the quality of life in their community in a way that concerns you?

What can you do to encourage these individuals to improve the quality of life in their community?

There is an old proverb that says, "You may not be able to change the world, but you can change the world for one person." Your community is your slice of the world, a slice that you can change dramatically for the people who live in it. However you define community—your neighborhood, an organization, or an alumni network—you can have an impact if you simply set some priorities and take action.

THROUGH THE LENS OF EXPERIENCE: *INSIGHTS ON WEALTH*

OPTIMIZE YOUR WEALTH:

I go and talk to kids in these programs—after-school programs, football kids, basketball, whatever. I love doing that. I love it because of the experience that I've had... I've been here, I left, and then I wanted to give up and come back. But I stayed out, went to college, played in the NFL, reached a pinnacle.

It's not enough just to have that type of wisdom and just keep it in and not be able to share it with the kids that kind of lived my life. I want to show them that it wasn't easy. It's about not giving up. Not giving up is how you reach wealth, and that's how you reach success, whatever it is to you.

Every kid has a dream, to me.

—Leigh Bodden, franchising entrepreneur and owner, Retro Fitness

Legacy Domain #6: The World at Large

	1	2	3	4	5	6	7	8	9	10
How concerned are you about the current state of the world at large?	1	2	3	4	5	6	7	8	9	10
How satisfied are you with your personal efforts to make a difference in the world at large?	1	2	3	4	5	6	7	8	9	10

In order of priority, list up to ten global causes or issues that you are most concerned about.

1.	6.
2.	7.
3.	8
4.	9.
5.	10.

What are you currently doing to support the efforts of those involved in addressing those causes or issues? Attach a separate sheet if necessary.

What else can you do to support the efforts of those involved in addressing those causes or issues?

Looking back, what could you have done differently as it relates to your contribution to the world at large?

Who among the people you care about is neglecting their personal contribution to the world at large?

What can you do to encourage these individuals to make a greater contribution to the world at large?

Once you have determined the impact that you want to make on your community or in the broader world, begin to outline the steps necessary to create that impact. As wealth managers, we often connect our clients to experts in various fields of nonprofit expertise to assist them in determining how to make gifts of both time and money to the communities and causes of their choice.

Legacy Domain #7: Your Financial Legacy

How important is your financial well-being as it relates to your personal legacy?	1	2	3	4	5	6	7	8	9	10
How satisfied are you with your current level of financial well-being?	1	2	3	4	5	6	7	8	9	10

Briefly describe how optimizing your financial well-being can help you create a more meaningful legacy?

Looking back, what could you have done differently in relation to optimizing your financial well-being?

Who among the people you care about is neglecting their financial well-being in a way that concerns you?

What can you do to encourage these individuals to manage their financial well-being more effectively or prudently?

Your financial legacy is a tangible tool that enables you to leave an imprint on the world. Whereas many people think that legacy planning begins and ends with planning your financial legacy, it is actually your thoughts about your legacy with respect to family, relationships, history and values, community, and the world that drives and determines your financial legacy. Your priorities for the nonfinancial legacy domains serve as your guide to allocating your financial resources in a manner that reflects your values.

Now that you have given thought to all of the legacy domains, take the following steps:

1. Select your top 3–5 legacy domains on which you would like to focus.

2. Select the top priorities from those domains.

3. Devise a few action steps for addressing those priorities. (And remember, getting help in figuring out the next step is a valid action step.)

4. Determine who else can help you with the action step.

We have provided a sample worksheet below, in addition to your blank worksheet.

Legacy Domain	Priorities	Action Step	Who Can Help Me
Health	Improve fitness	Exercise for 35 minutes per day	Get Max to walk with me
	Enhance diet	Eat fewer carbs	Buy low-carb cookbook
Knowledge	Firsthand knowledge of teachers and their use of the Internet	Develop business idea	Put together focus group of ten teachers
Community	Address educational disparities in low-income neighborhoods in my community	Start an educational foundation	Meet with school district officials to identify local project needs

History/values	Expand family genealogical knowledge	Extend the family tree on Great-Great-Grandma's side	Aunt Ginny, who has done the initial research
	Learn Southern cooking	Have gumbo and jambalaya sessions with Mom	Mom
Financial	Start new venture	Write business plan	Inc.com website
	Start educational foundation	Set up nonprofit organization	Local nonprofit consultant

Your Worksheet

Legacy Domain	Priorities	Action Step	Who Can Help Me

By employing the principles outlined in this book, you will be equipped to build a rich, fulfilling life and a meaningful, sustainable legacy. Do not be concerned if your legacy planning is much simpler or far more complex than this sample. Remember, this process is all about *your* plan and *you* making your wishes come true with *your* legacy. There are no right or wrong answers—only *your* answers.

Optimizing the dimension of Legacy Planning is where this exercise and your team of experts come in. For many, this dimension of wealth is one of the most important. As a wealth advisor, the exploration of a client's desired legacy is crucial in giving me insight into a client's driving force.

By having a team and a thoughtful, integrated, written plan, you can easily make changes as your goals—or the people involved in your goals—change. Then each change becomes only a slight revision rather than a total remake of your plan. In my wealth management practice, I live by the principle of "Do it right the first time." Yes, things change, but the more thought that goes into the plan, the greater the accuracy and the better the results.

Also, you never know when the plan will have to take effect, since life is short. This process is about being prepared so that you can leave your legacy…your way. As a wealth management professional, I know from experience with clients that bedside estate plans are not the plans that you want to have if you want a meaningful legacy!

CHAPTER 9

Build Your Team

One of the first things you should consider as you look to build your team is what each member can bring to the table. Even if you *think* you understand the difference between the six basic groups of investment professionals listed in Chapter 4, it would behoove you to do a little research. Some of their descriptions, who regulates them, and what they actually offer their clients may surprise you.

There are many different definitions of what each investment professional is and what their expertise is, so be prepared for different sources to say different things. You can also go to the regulatory body of each profession. For example, for an insurance agent, go to the state insurance department's site; for a CPA, go to the state's board of accountancy; for an attorney, go to the state bar; for stockbrokers and investment advisors, go to the FINRA and SEC sites. You will find that having the definitions will give you a quick look at the profession in general but very little help in the areas of specialty. In the reference section of this book is a list of designations that one can obtain, and the list is quite long. I have had many people tell me that trying to find out what each professional does and what that means is quite overwhelming, and I concur.

So you can use the reference at the end of the book for a quick look, but my suggestion is that when it comes to picking your team, let your trusted advisor help you select the proper areas of expertise needed for the team. Think about this: attorneys have different specialties just as medical doctors do. You would not want a dentist doing colon surgery or an insurance agent giving you legal advice about your divorce. This is an extreme example, but I think you get the picture.

When you are building your team, you have unique circumstances and goals, and you need a team to be your specialists. Many times, the planner or wealth advisor is the leader of your team after yourself, having the knowledge and experience to help you select experts in the areas you need. Just imagine if you had to understand all the different letters and designations of each profession—that alone would be overwhelming. Now add to that their areas of specialization, their personalities, and how they work as a team. Many advisors do not like to work as a team, preferring to do the work themselves. If your personalities and learning styles are extremely different, you may have trouble communicating with a particular advisor. He may talk the entire time you are there while you have no idea what he is saying, or he may seem to prefer to talk over your head to impress you.

How do you feel if someone talks down to you? Have you ever had that experience? I have, and I didn't like it at all. It seemed the other person was too busy for me and my questions, like he or she just wanted my money and for me to leave as soon as possible. When it comes to money, most people have a limited time to enjoy their assets and goals, and they need the money to do what they want it to do and be there when they need it. If the advisor and client cannot get on the same page quickly, can you imagine what your money will look like in 5, 10, or 20 years? For each prospective team member, ask yourself if he or she would really place your best interests ahead of theirs. All the designations and awards in the world cannot make a bad team member a good match for your wealth plan.

In picking your team, get a leader who has your interests at heart over someone with super impressive numbers. Your personality type will influence you to some degree in the types of people you choose for your team—another reason I stress understanding yourself and your money, so that you are aware of your own decision-making positives and negatives. That understanding can aid you greatly in future decisions and help you optimize your wealth and see potential pitfalls.

The most important thing is having a leader with honor and integrity so that when it comes to you and what he or she does for you, their moral compass never strays. It seems that those words are used like confetti and are everywhere, but many times they do not truly come from the heart. They are simply used to enhance business. I know what it is like to take a handshake as gospel and to lose everything I worked for as a result, but still I truly believe that honor and integrity should guide how we conduct our lives and our businesses. I wish it were that easy. Money can bring out the best and worst in people. So I wish you a lot of luck in finding the best people for your situation. If you take positive steps and build a great team, you will have several professionals working together and keeping an eye on each other as well—not just knowing each other through professional courtesy but actually as team players for your best interests.

Getting Background Information
on Financial Advisor(s)

Before selecting a financial professional, ask the questions outlined in Chapter 3, Check Your Assumptions. You also need to conduct your own investigation using the resources outlined below.

Brokers and Brokerage Firms

FINRA Broker Check is a free tool that allows investors to check the professional background of brokerage firms and brokers currently or formerly registered with FINRA or a national securities exchange, as well as current or former investment advisor firms and representatives. Broker Check information is drawn from filings by regulators, firms, and investment professionals. It includes current licensing status and history, employment history, and, if any, reported regulatory, customer dispute, criminal, and other matters.

Through Broker Check, you can:

- Search for information about brokers and brokerage firms

- Search for information about investment advisor firms and representatives

- Obtain online background reports, if available

- Link to additional resources such as educational tools for investors

Investment Advisors

Some investment advisors and their representatives appear in Broker Check because they are also registered as or associated with broker-dealers. However, to do a thorough check of any investment advisor, you should ask for—and carefully read—the firm's registration document or "Form ADV." Form ADV is a form that investment advisors must file with the SEC or the state securities agency in the state where the firm has its principal place of business. The form includes the following:

- Information about the advisory firm's business

- Record of any problems with regulators or clients in the past

- Services, fees, and investment strategies.

Investment advisors must register with either the SEC or a state securities regulator, depending on the amount of client assets they manage. Generally, only larger advisors that have $25 million or more of assets under management or that provide advice to investment company clients are permitted to register with the SEC. Smaller advisors register under state law with state securities authorities.[1] Although the SEC does not separately register individual representatives of investment advisory firms, many states do.

Form ADV has two parts. Part 1 has information about the advisory firm's business and whether they've had problems with regulators or clients in the past. Part 2 describes their services, fees, and investment strategies. Before you hire an investment advisory firm, examine both parts of Form ADV, and then ask for an explanation of anything you don't understand. You should be offered a copy of the ADV before or at the time you choose to do business with them, as well.

In addition to asking the firm for a copy, you will be able to find an advisory firm's most recent Form ADV online through FINRA Broker Check or the SEC's Investment Advisor Public Disclosure (IAPD) website. You can also obtain information about investment advisor representatives through FINRA's Broker Check, the SEC's IAPD website, or by contacting your state securities regulator.

Resources for Other Investment Professionals
Apart from FINRA Broker Check and the SEC's IAPD database, you can get licensing information for other types of investment professionals as follows:

Type of Professional	Licensing Body or Regulator
Accountant	State board of accountancy
Lawyer	State bar association
Insurance agent	State insurance commission
Financial planner	Confirm whether the planner is licensed by or registered with the SEC, FINRA, or a state regulator and check with that regulator
Broker	FINRA

Remember to do the best you can, but even the best credentials do not guarantee you the best advice for you or your situation. I always tell people to trust their gut sometimes as well. Having a trustworthy advisor with your best interests at heart could mean years of peace of mind, knowing someone truly "has your back"!

1 General Information on the Regulation of Investment Advisers. *Division of Investment Management.* U.S. Securities and Exchange Commission, n.d. Web. 04 Feb. 2015.

CONCLUSION

By reading this book, you have taken the first step in building a wealth plan. You are now positioned to not merely manage your money but to manage your wealth—*your personal concept* of wealth. Managing your wealth requires an entirely different level of thought and expertise than simply managing money.

Managing your wealth is challenging because everything is in constant flux all around us. It takes a lot of expertise and good decisions to stay on track, especially when the track keeps moving. If you really want to make a difference, and if you want to take positive steps in helping yourself, your family, and your legacy, then you are now on the right track.

You have learned that becoming more financially literate is only the first part of a successful wealth management plan. Your mind and your emotions will act like little gremlins trying to steer you in the wrong direction.

"Knowing thyself" can help you avoid missteps such as managing investments in the same way you manage a retirement plan or including an individual in your legacy plan who lacks sound judgment. Knowing thyself is crucial, because as you get older you have less time to recover from those missteps.

The crux of your strategy is to build a team—with a great team leader—to help you build your optimized wealth plan. Smart, successful people always try to surround themselves with smarter people, and so should you. Each member of your team will play a key role in managing the Eight Dimensions of Wealth. Simply having a team on your side that can take an integrative approach to your wealth will set you apart from many people.

But choose your team carefully. Many financial professionals simply want to manage your investment portfolio. They give little or no attention to the many other vital areas of your optimized wealth plan.

Wealth is a journey. So, no matter where you are in your journey, I wish you a wonderfully fulfilling trip that will help your dreams come true. If you can take at least one tip from this book, the book will pay for itself again and again for a lifetime—and perhaps for the lifetime of another generation.

REFERENCE

Just a few of the financial advisor designations out there:

DESIGNATION / TITLE	ACRONYM
3 Dimensional Wealth Practitioner	3DWP
Accredited Advisor in Insurance	AAI
Accredited Asset Management Specialist	AAMS
Accredited Domestic Partnership Advisor	ADPA
Accredited Estate Planner	AEP
Accredited Financial Counselor	AFC
Accredited Investment Fiduciary	AIF
Accredited Investment Fiduciary Analyst	AIFA
Accredited Pension Representative	APR
Accredited Portfolio Management Advisor	APMA
Accredited Retirement Plan Consultant	ARPC
Accredited Tax Advisor	ATA
Accredited Tax Preparer	ATP
Accredited Wealth Management Advisor	AWMA
Asset Protection Planner	APP
Associate in General Insurance	AINS (formerly INS)
Associate in Insurance Services	AIS
Associate in Personal Insurance	API
Associate, Financial Services Institute	AFSI
Associate, Life Management Institute	ALMI
Board Certified in Annuities	BCA
Board Certified in Asset Allocation	BCAA

Board Certified in Estate Planning	BCE
Board Certified in Mutual Funds	BCM
Board Certified in Securities	BCS
Certified 401(k) Professional	C(k)P
Certified AML Specialist	CAMLS
Certified Annuity Advisor	CAA
Certified Annuity Consultant	CAC
Certified Annuity Specialist	CAS
Certified Anti-Money Laundering Specialist	CAMS
Certified Asset Protection Planner	CAPP
Certified College Planning Specialist	CCPS
Certified Compliance Specialist	CCOS
Certified Credit Counselor	CCC
Certified Divorce Financial Analyst	CDFA
Certified Divorce Planner	CDP
Certified Educator in Personal Finance	CEPF
Certified Elder Planning Specialist	CEPS
Certified Employee Benefit Specialist	CEBS
Certified Equity Indexed Annuity Specialist	CEIAS
Certified Estate Advisor	CEA
Certified Estate Planner	CEP
Certified Estate and Trust Specialist (formerly Board Certified in Estate Planning)	CES
Certified Exit Planner	CExP
Certified Exit Planning Advisor	CEPA
Certified Financial Consultant	CFC
Certified Financial Divorce Practitioner	CFDP
Certified Financial Educator	CFEd
Certified Financial Gerontologist	CFG
Certified Financial Marketing Professional	CFMP
Certified Financial Planner	CFP
Certified Financial Wellness Educator	CFWE

Certified Fund Specialist	CFS
Certified IRA Services Professional	CISP
Certified Income Specialist (formerly Retirement Income Specialist)	CIS (formerly RIS)
Certified Insurance Service Representative	CISR
Certified Investment Management Analyst	CIMA
Certified Investment Management Consultant	CIMC
Certified Long-Term Care	CLTC
Certified Merger and Acquisition Advisor	CMAA
Certified Pension Consultant	CPC
Certified Personal Banker	CPB
Certified Personal Finance Counselor	CPFC
Certified Portfolio Specialist	CPS
Certified Private Wealth Advisor	CPWA
Certified Professional Insurance Agent	CPIA
Certified Professional Insurance Woman/Man	CPIW/M
Certified Public Accountant	CPA
Certified Retirement Administrator	CRA
Certified Retirement Counselor	CRC
Certified Retirement Financial Advisor	CRFA
Certified Retirement Planner	CRP
Certified Retirement Services Professional	CRSP
Certified Senior Advisor	CSA
Certified Senior Consultant	CSC
Certified Specialist in Estate Planning	CSEP
Certified Specialist in Retirement Planning	CSRP
Certified Tax Specialist	CTS
Certified Treasury Professional	CTP
Certified Trust and Financial Advisor	CTFA
Certified Wealth Consultant	CWC
Certified Wealth Management Specialist	CWMS
Certified Wealth Preservation Planner	CWPP

Certified Wealth Smart Strategist	CWSS
Certified Wealth Strategist	CWS
Certified Workplace Money Coach	CWMC
Chartered Advisor for Senior Living	CASL
Chartered Advisor in Philanthropy	CAP
Chartered Alternative Investment Analyst	CAIA
Chartered Asset Manager	CAM
Chartered Estate Planning Practitioner	CEPP
Chartered Federal Employee Benefits Consultant	ChFEBC
Chartered Financial Analyst	CFA
Chartered Financial Consultant	ChFC
Chartered Financial Engineer	ChFE
Chartered Investment Counselor	CIC
Chartered Life Underwriter	CLU
Chartered Market Analyst	CMA
Chartered Market Technician	CMT
Chartered Mutual Fund Counselor	CMFC
Chartered Portfolio Manager	CPM
Chartered Private Wealth Advisor	CPWA
Chartered Property Casualty Underwriter	CPCU
Chartered Retirement Planning Counselor	CRPC
Chartered Retirement Plans Specialist	CRPS
Chartered Senior Financial Planner	CSFP
Chartered Trust and Estate Planner	CTEP
Chartered Wealth Manager	CWM
Christian Financial Professionals Network Certified Member	CFPN
Direct Participation Professional	DPP
Disability Income Associate	DIA
Diversified Advanced Education	DAE
Employee Healthcare Benefits Associate	EHBA
Endorsed Local Provider	ELP
Enrolled Agent	EA

Fellow of the Academy of Life Underwriting	FALU
Fellow, Financial Services Institute	FFSI
Fellow, Life Management Institute	FLMI
Financial Analyst Designate	FAD or CMA
Financial Risk Manager	FRM
Financial Services Specialist	FSS
Fraternal Insurance Counselor	FIC
Fraternal Insurance Counselor Fellow	FICF
Global Fiduciary Strategist	GFS
Life Underwriter Training Council Fellow	LUTCF
Master Certified Estate Planner	MCEP
Master Financial Professional	MFP
PLANSPONSOR Retirement Professional	PRP
Personal Financial Specialist	PFS
Personal Retirement Planning Specialist	PRPS
Professional Plan Consultant	PPC
Qualified Financial Planner	QFP
Qualified Kingdom Advisor	QKA
Qualified Plan Financial Consultant	QPFC
Registered Fiduciary	RF
Registered Financial Associate	RFA
Registered Financial Consultant	RFC
Registered Financial Gerontologist	RFG
Registered Financial Planner	RFP
Registered Financial Specialist	RFS
Registered Paraplanner	RP
Retirement Income Certified Professional	RICP
Retirement Income Specialist	RIS
Retirement Management Analyst	RMA
Retirement Plans Associate	RPA
Wealth Management Specialist	WMS

Industry associations:

Alliance of American Insurers

American Bankers Association

American Benefits Council

American Council of Life Insurers

American Countertrade Association

American Insurance Association

Emerging Markets Private Equity Association

Equipment Leasing and Finance Association

Finance, Credit & International Business

Investment Company Institute

Latin American Venture Capital Association

Mortgage Bankers Association

National Association of Insurance Commissioners

National Venture Capital Association

Property Casualty Insurers Association of America

Reinsurance Association of America

Securities Industry and Financial Markets Association

Small Business Investor Alliance

Industry publications:

American Banker

Bloomberg BusinessWeek

Global Finance

Institutional Investor

Mortgage Banking

Pensions & Investments

The Wall Street Journal

CONTRIBUTORS

The following profiles provide background information on the contributors to "Through the Lens of Experience: Insights on Wealth."

Omar Ashmawy

A first generation American—the son of Italian and Egyptian immigrants—Omar was born and raised in New Jersey. After graduating law school from George Washington University, he served eight years as an active duty officer in the US Air Force.

He has a lifelong passion for the environment, believing that sustainable development of our communities is the key to long-term, successful economic and cultural growth. The PlayGreen Initiative was, in part, an idea born of his childhood experiences in urban New Jersey and his time living in rural North Dakota as an air force officer.

Omar volunteers his legal and logistical expertise to PGI because he believes our future depends on a meaningful respect for our children and our world. In his day job, he serves as one of the youngest staff directors and chief counsels for a committee in the US House of Representatives.

Leigh Bodden

Leigh Bodden is the founder and CEO of the WEOU Group, LLC. Leigh started the company toward the tail end of his NFL career as a way of transferring the leadership he exhibited on the gridiron into the next chapter of his life in the business world. As a player, Leigh had the reputation of being a physical and intelligent defensive back. As an entrepreneur, he is leveraging his will to win as well as his educational background. Leigh holds a bachelor's degree in business management from Duquesne University and is currently pursuing an executive MBA from George Washington University School of Business.

Leigh is very active in the community. He founded the Leigh Bodden Foundation in 2010 to support the development of well-rounded youth in the Washington, DC metropolitan area. The mission of the Leigh Bodden Foundation is to encourage and guide youth to focus on increasing their personal knowledge, improving their physical well-being, and expanding their horizons, thereby empowering them to transform their hopes and dreams into real possibilities.

The WEOU Group is currently focused on franchise acquisitions. In 2013, the company signed a deal with fitness company

Retro Fitness (www.RetroFitness.com) to become its lead franchise developer in the Washington, DC metropolitan area.

Molly Dworken Herman

Molly Dworken Herman was born and raised in the Washington, DC metropolitan area. Over the past 15 years, Molly has focused her career on improving the lives of seniors on a local, state, and national level.

Currently, she is employed by RealPage, Inc., where she has spent the last five years developing partnerships with senior care providers and building both internal and external sales teams.

Other noteworthy organizations she has worked with include A Place for Mom, the National Council on Aging, Leading Age, and Sunrise Senior Living. Molly and her husband, Robert Herman, reside in Kensington, Maryland, and became parents to their first son, Edison, in March of 2014

Christopher A. Moeller, MD

Christopher Moeller has been in private practice since 1987 and practice director of the Skin Enhancement Center since 2001. Dr. Moeller and his staff care for dermatological diseases affecting the skin, hair, and nails and specialize in skin cancer treatments and cosmetic treatments.

He also is a clinical assistant professor in the Department of Internal Medicine at the University of Kansas School of Medicine and is an adjunct professor at the School of Health Sciences at Wichita State University.

A graduate of Duke University, Dr. Moeller is a diplomat of the American Board of Dermatology, a fellow of the American Academy of Dermatology, a fellow of the American Society for Mohs Surgery, a fellow of the American Society of Dermatological Surgery, a member of the American Society for Laser Medicine and Surgery, and a member of the American Society of Cosmetic Dermatology and Aesthetic Surgery.

Lisa Spoden

Lisa Spoden is president of Strategic Implementation Solutions (SIS). She works with a number of companies, including Burkman and Associates, and is a partner at I do I don't Worldwide. She has a PhD and MS in health services administration. Her strategic planning and program development expertise is coupled with practical management know-how, having previously worked as a senior executive at hospitals and medical group practices.

Lisa also owned and developed Strategic Health Care (SHC), where she is still senior vice president. SHC works with health-care provider groups in the areas of managed care negotiations, association management, grant writing/management, government relations, and policy development.

Her community involvement currently includes: board of directors at the College of St. Benedict, board of advisors at Shenandoah University, Aurora Foundation board, Great Falls

Friends and Neighbors president, and We Will Survive Cancer board. She has previously been involved in the National Association of Hospice and Palliative Care, American Cancer Society, and United Way boards as well as a Boy Scouts of America medical explorer post leader, chamber of commerce goodwill ambassador, and Junior Achievement advisor.

Lisa has authored and been quoted in many articles for professional journals. She wrote "Managed Care Contracting Survival Guide for Providers," which was released in the fall of 2007 for HCPro, and "End of Life Care in Kentucky," for which she was presented the Kentucky colonel recognition by the governor. Lisa was honored as "Entrepreneur of the Year" by the College of St. Benedict and St. John's University in 2013.

ABOUT THE AUTHOR

Since 1986, Stan Webb has been a steady beacon in a world filled with complexity and uncertainty. In addition to obtaining his professional securities licenses, Stan is a certified fund specialist and a certified senior advisor. He attained these designations in order to better help his clients achieve their financial goals and objectives. However, it is his passion for helping people that may set him apart from other financial professionals.

Stan's personal mission of serving others began to develop as a child. He grew up in a working-class family and saw his parents struggle firsthand. While they knew very little about investing, they instilled in him a set of core values that now enable him to establish long-standing relationships that span multiple generations with his clients.

In addition to helping his clients optimize their wealth, Stan is active in his community, serving as a strong advocate for financial literacy as well as the host of DreamCatcher Radio. He helps families confront the many challenges of aging with his Eldercare Channel of Wichita. He also works tirelessly to help children learn about money so that they can be effective wealth stewards when they become adults.

Contact Stan Webb for more information on...

- Dynamic Wealth Management™

- Eldercare Planning

- Portfolio Management

- Education

- Financial Literacy

WWW.STANTWEBB.COM

DREAMCATCHER WEALTH MANAGEMENT

300 N. MAIN STREET
SUITE 309
WICHITA, KANSAS 67202
316.265.5151

Printed in the USA
CPSIA information can be obtained
at www.ICGtesting.com
JSHW012055140824
68134JS00035B/3444